THE

George W. Bush Quiz Book

Also by Paul Slansky

The Clothes Have No Emperor

Dan Quayle: Airhead Apparent
(co-written with Steve Radlauer)

THE

George W. Bush
Quiz Book

PAUL SLANSKY

BROADWAY BOOKS NEW YORK

BROADWAY

Broadway Books titles may be purchased for business or promotional use
or for special sales. For information, please write to: Special Markets
Department, Random House, Inc., 1745 Broadway, New York, NY 10019.

PRINTED IN THE UNITED STATES OF AMERICA

BROADWAY BOOKS and its logo, a letter B bisected on the
diagonal, are trademarks of Random House, Inc.

Visit our website at www.broadwaybooks.com

First edition published 2004.
Portions of this book originally appeared in *The New Yorker*.

Updates to this book will be posted periodically throughout the campaign
at www.thegeorgebushquizbook.com.

Book design by Laurie Jewell
Title page photograph by Rick Wilking/REUTERS

Library of Congress Cataloging-in-Publication Data

Slansky, Paul
    The George W. Bush quiz book / Paul Slansky.
        p. cm.
        1. Bush, George W. (George Walker), 1946—Miscellanea.
2. Presidents—United States—Biography—Miscellanea. I. Title.

F903.3 S57 2004
973.931'092—dc22

                                                    2004040751

ISBN 0-7679-1784-7

10 9 8 7 6 5 4 3 2 1

For Liz and Grace,

who endure him with me.

Contents

Quiz #1

Growing Up Bush

Boy George

1. What *was not* a favorite pastime of George W. Bush as a young boy?

   A. Playing baseball
   B. Reading books
   C. Collecting baseball cards
   D. Blowing up frogs with firecrackers

ANSWER: B. He very much enjoyed each of the other activities.

2. What was George W. Bush's response when, during a campaign photo opportunity at a South Carolina elementary school, a student asked him what his favorite book was as a child?

1

A. "We're just takin' pictures now, we're not takin' questions."

B. "The one about that little monkey George. You know, some people think I look a little chimpy."

C. "I can't remember any specific books."

D. *Lord of the Flies.* And my favorite part was when they killed the fat kid."

ANSWER: C. He couldn't remember a single book.

3. What happened when his mother took thirteen-year-old George W. Bush and his friend Doug Hannah to play golf at her Houston country club?

A. Young George W. got caught sneaking a beer.

B. The boys drove a golf cart into a water trap.

C. Young George W. got upset when he failed to tee off well and started screaming, "Fuck this," after which his mother told him to go sit in the car.

D. The boys got caught killing frogs.

ANSWER: C. This happened more than once, and Doug Hannah recalls Bush as quite the sore loser. "If you were playing basketball and you were playing to eleven and he was down, you went to fifteen," Hannah told *Vanity Fair's* Gail Sheehy. "If he wasn't winning, he would quit. He would just walk off. It's what we called Bush Effort: If I don't like the game, I take my ball and go home." On one occasion Barbara Bush told Hannah his friend George W. was going to have "optical rectosis."

4. According to Barbara Bush, what did "optical rectosis" mean?

A. "A nervous eye tic that shows up when you're angry, which George is all the time."

B. "A bad eye smell."

2

C. "An inability to see things clearly."

D. "A shitty outlook on life."

5. Much of George W. Bush's life has been spent following in his father's footsteps but having trouble filling them, a tradition that began at the exclusive Phillips Academy at Andover. Bush's father was captain of the school's baseball team. How did George W. underachieve him?

A. He was merely a better than average player and never made captain.

B. He was so determined to excel that he injured himself in the tryouts and never made the team.

C. He became captain of the badminton team.

D. Instead of actually playing a sport, he became captain of the cheerleading team.

Boola George

6. How did George W. Bush recall the experience of going to Yale during a time of antiwar protest, urban riots, and general social upheaval?

A. "For me it was really four years of nonstop booze and sports."

B. "The sixties—what a lousy time to be in college."

C. "I don't remember any kind of heaviness ruining my time at Yale."

D. "Protest, shmotest. Riots, shmiots. Upheaval, shmupheaval. I didn't give a damn about any of that."

ANSWER: C. No heaviness and no academic excellence—in four years, not a single A.

7. When did George W. Bush say he stopped liking the Beatles?

A. When they "kicked out Pete Best."
B. When they "went through kind of a weird psychedelic period, which I didn't particularly care for."
C. When John Lennon "stood there naked on that album cover next to that ugly Japanese chick Yono."
D. "When Paul died."

ANSWER: B.

8. When George W. Bush pledged to the super-secret ultra-elite Yale club Skull & Bones, this now-compulsive giver of nicknames was unable to come up with a secret name for himself. TRUE OR FALSE?

ANSWER: **True.** They dubbed him "Temporary," and he never bothered to change the name.

9. What did George W. Bush resent about Yale?

A. That it waited until 1991 to give his father an honorary degree.
B. The decision by left-leaning documentary filmmaker Helen Whitney, the wife of its president,

Benno C. Schmidt Jr., not to attend the overdue reception for his father.

C. Its chaplain, William Sloane Coffin Jr., having said to him at the time of his father's loss to Ralph Yarborough in a 1964 Texas Senate race, "I know your father. Frankly, he was beaten by a better man."

D. All of the above.

ANSWER: D. He also hated how so many of the students seemed to feel guilty about being rich.

10. Scott Armstrong, a Yale classmate, recalls George W. Bush as "the hailest fellow you'd ever well meet, just a prince of a guy." TRUE OR FALSE?

ANSWER: False. Armstrong described Bush as "someone who looked like he had an inside joke that no one gets or cares about."

11. For what was George W. Bush first arrested?

A. Pulling down the goalposts after a Yale-Princeton football game

B. Stealing a Christmas wreath from a New Haven hotel

C. Dancing naked atop a bar at Yale

D. Possession of cocaine

ANSWER B. He was not arrested for his part in the football melee (but was told to waste no time getting out of Princeton). Rumors persist that a photo exists of a nude bar dance, but if so it has yet to surface—as does any corroboration of rumors of a 1972 coke bust.

12. Not only was George W. Bush an enthusiastic participant in the branding of new pledges to his jock frat,

5

Deke, with a hot coat hanger, but he actually defended the practice in his earliest appearance in the national press, an article in *The New York Times* in which he explained that the resulting injury was no worse than "a cigarette burn" that left "no scarring mark physically or mentally." TRUE OR FALSE?

ANSWER: True.

Quiz #2

The Extended Adolescence

Getting Out of 'Nam

1. What was George W. Bush's response to a reporter's query as to whether he had joined the Texas Air National Guard in order to stay out of Vietnam?

A. "It wasn't about not going to Vietnam per se so much as it was not wanting to get killed or lose any limbs. It wouldn't have mattered where the war was."

B. "Maybe I did, maybe I didn't. What's the relevance?"

C. "Hell, no. Do you think I'm going to admit that?"

D. "Did you volunteer? Show me *your* war wounds."

ANSWER: C. "Maybe I did, maybe I didn't. What's the relevance?" was his answer to the question of whether he'd ever used illegal drugs.

2. Though former Guard officials clearly recall a long waiting list at the time, George W. Bush maintains that "they were having trouble getting people to volunteer to go to pilot school" and that no strings needed to be pulled to get him out of the draft and into the National Guard. TRUE OR FALSE?

3. Who is Ben Barnes?

A. The then-speaker of the Texas House of Representatives who said he pulled strings to get George W. Bush into the National Guard.
B. The Maine police officer who pulled George W. Bush over one night in September 1976 and found him to have been driving drunk.
C. A boyhood friend of George W. Bush's who described him as "not contemplative or reflective. He's not a guy who would go off by himself thinking of something. He's more likely to be hiding in a tree to jump down on somebody."
D. George W. Bush's psychiatrist.

The "Nomadic Years"

4. Complete George W. Bush's description of his behavior during the extended-by-decades adolescence that he refers to as his "nomadic years": "When I was young and irresponsible, I _____"

A. failed to report for National Guard duty and got away with it.

B. had several run-ins with the law.

C. was young and irresponsible.

D. was a really obnoxious drunk.

ANSWER: C. All the answers are true, though the others don't complete this particular off-stated quote.

5. George W. Bush took Harvard Business School seriously enough to start wearing a jacket and tie to class for the first time in his academic career. TRUE OR FALSE?

ANSWER: False. He sat in the back of the classroom wearing his National Guard bomber jacket and spitting tobacco juice into a Styrofoam cup, or chewing gum and blowing bubbles, or dipping snuff. According to a fellow student, "He was so juvenile! He actually threw spitballs in class."

6. What changed in George W. Bush's life after he married Laura?

A. His mean streak melted away virtually overnight.

B. He stopped using words incorrectly.

C. He found that he'd lost the taste for alcohol.

D. He stopped bringing his laundry over to his friends' houses for their wives to wash.

ANSWER: D.

7. What faux pas did George W. Bush commit during his losing 1978 race for a West Texas congressional seat?

A. He tried to convey how energetic he was in a TV spot by jogging, an activity then quite alien to Texans.

B. He tried to entice Texas Tech students to support him by serving them beer at a campaign party.

C. He showed up at a candidate forum on a farm and blithely announced, "Today is the first time I've been on a real farm."

D. All of the above.

ANSWER: D.

8. What did his closest friends call George W. Bush during those "nomadic years"?

A. "Bushie"
B. "The Bombastic Bushkin"
C. "The Arrogant Arbusto"
D. "Gweeb"

ANSWER B. Laura calls him Bushie. Arbusto (Spanish for Bush) was the name of his first oil company. And he seems like a guy who'd ask you to step outside if you called him Gweeb.

9. Why did George W. Bush change the name of his oil company from Arbusto to Bush Exploration?

A. His mother told him to.
B. It turned out there already was an Arbusto.
C. Though it was actually pronounced "Ar-*boost*-o," people had taken to calling it "Ar-*bust*-o," as in busted.
D. He decided he wanted to have a company with the word "oil" in the title, then forgot to put it in.

ANSWER: C.

10. Complete George W. Bush's recollection of trying to build up his various oil businesses, which ranged from not particularly successful to failing (though somehow he always got bailed out by his father's buddies, who got to take huge tax write-offs): "I became totally _____ with hitting the big one."

A. obsessed
B. consumed
C. preoccupied
D. inebriated

ANSWER: D.

Booze

11. How old was George W. Bush when, confronted by his father for driving home so drunk that he crashed into a neighbor's garbage can, he blurted, "I hear you're lookin' for me. You wanna go mano a mano right here?"

A. Seventeen
B. Nineteen
C. Twenty-six
D. Thirty-nine

ANSWER: C. No fisticuffs ensued, however, but as Bush's sister Dorothy, who witnessed the incident, recalled, "My dad was not happy. My dad did not think that was attractive or funny or nice."

12. In the spring of 1986, *The Washingtonian* ran a feature in which various pundits predicted the next Republican presidential nominee. (Half named Vice President George H. W. Bush, half named someone else.) Which journalist (who picked someone else) was confronted in a Dallas restaurant by the Vice President's defender, his drunken son, George W. who, in front of the journalist's wife and four-year-old son, said, "You no good fucking son-of-a-bitch, I will never fucking forget what you wrote"?

A. Fred Barnes of *The New Republic.*
B. Al Hunt of *The Wall Street Journal.*
C. George Will of *The Washington Post.*
D. Thomas DeFrank of *Newsweek.*

ANSWER: B. Bush confronted DeFrank the following year, after *Newsweek* ran a cover story on the "Wimp Factor" in his father's campaign, phoning him to say, "Tommy, I've got bad news. *Newsweek*'s been cut off. You're out of business."

13. Which of his then-teenage siblings were in the car with George W. Bush for his two most famous drunk-driving episodes—the aforementioned garbage can incident and his renowned DUI arrest?

A. Neil and Jeb
B. Dorothy and Marvin
C. Jeb and Dorothy
D. Marvin and Neil

ANSWER: B. Marvin, then sixteen, was with him when he crashed into the garbage can, and Dorothy, then seventeen, was with him when he got busted.

14. Which future cabinet member was with George W. Bush on his fortieth birthday weekend when he decided to stop drinking?

A. HUD secretary Mel Martinez
B. Commerce secretary Donald L. Evans

C. Education secretary Rod Paige

D. Secretary of State Colin Powell

ANSWER: B.

15. How much time passed between George W. Bush's Maine arrest for drunk driving and his realization that he needed to stop drinking, period?

A. Two minutes

B. Five days

C. Six weeks

D. Ten years

ANSWER: D. DUI at thirty, drying out at forty. And even then, it wouldn't have happened without dozens of "booze or me" ultimatums from Laura.

Quiz #3

The Late Blooming

The First First Son

1. How did George W. Bush deal with an openly flirtatious coworker on his father's 1988 presidential campaign?

A. He had her transferred to another office.

B. He tried to discourage her by spitting tobacco juice into a Styrofoam cup whenever she was in the same room.

C. He called her into his office and gently told her he wasn't interested.

D. He told her off in a humiliating manner and, when a campaign official told him "You really hurt her," he replied, "Good, good. I'm a married man. I'm glad she got the signal."

ANSWER: D.

14

2. How did Bill Kristol, who served at the time as Dan Quayle's chief of staff, describe his experiences with George W. Bush in his father's White House?

   A. "The nicest guy you'd ever want to meet. We always looked forward to his visits."
   B. "He always had this expression on his face like he was smelling shit. God, how we hated him."
   C. "It really gave me some insight into how Quayle got picked in the first place. Obviously, he reminded the old man of his son, only without the dry drunk personality."
   D. "He was fine . . . well, I don't know if he was fine. He was actually kind of a jackass, but . . . he was the president's kid."

ANSWER: D.

3. What was George W. Bush's expression for the blistering tongue-lashings he gave people whom he felt were insufficiently loyal to, or respectful of, his father?

   A. "Bush bashing"
   B. "Losing it"
   C. "Feisting out"
   D. "Sticking it in"

ANSWER: C.

4. According to Richard Ben Cramer's book *What It Takes,* George W. Bush showed up at a 1986 baseball playoff game at the Houston Astrodome expecting to sit with his parents. Instead, they were led off to the owner's box, and George W. and his party were taken to seats he considered inferior. When he looked over and saw his father's chief of staff, Craig Fuller, sitting with his dad—in the seat that should have been his!—he flipped out and charged over to the owner's box, where, in response to political consultant Lee Atwater's casual "What's happening?" he snarled loudly, *"How the hell would I know? Seats ain't worth a shit. I guess the box got a little* crowded . . . *People who think they gotta be here."* TRUE OR FALSE?

5. Complete Andrew Card's assessment of George W. Bush's demeanor during his stint as troubleshooter on his father's 1988 presidential campaign: "He was kind of a quiet enforcer. He was there to observe and make sure loose cannons weren't rolling around the deck. When he wasn't happy, _____"

A. he did a good job of hiding it.
B. sparks would fly.
C. it was pretty easy to find out that he wasn't happy.
D. he tended to talk about how much he missed drinking.

6. At a White House state dinner for the Queen of England, First Lady Barbara Bush sat her forty-two-year-old son George W. at the opposite end of the table from the guest of honor "for fear of him saying something." TRUE OR FALSE?

7. What family dispute was Rev. Billy Graham called upon to settle?

   A. George W. Bush wanted his brother Marvin to give back the leather-bound collection of autographed baseball cards that he had given him years earlier, and Marvin refused.

   B. George W. Bush said that only people who accepted Christ as their savior could get into Heaven, and his mother disagreed.

   C. Jeb Bush, who would frequently say, "I'm not running for governor because I'm George and Barbara's son. I'm running because I'm George P. and Noelle and Jebbie's father," was furious at George W. for stealing the line and adapting it for his own gubernatorial campaign.

   D. Jenna Bush's anti–death penalty position vs. George W. Bush's rather more pro-execution stance.

ANSWER: **B.** Graham basically sided with George W. Bush, but ceded the final decision to God.

8. Although accusations of insider trading were made against George W. Bush in connection with his dumping most of his stock in Harken Energy (the company that had bailed out *his* company) two months before it posted a $20 million loss, what may have been a deciding factor in the SEC's failure to file charges against him?

   A. SEC chairman Richard Breeden was a former aide to Bush's father.

   B. SEC general counsel John Doty was a former lawyer to Bush's father.

C. Bush's father was president at the time.

D. All of the above.

ANSWER: D. There's so much that's shady about this deal. SEC records show that Bush, as a company director, had been warned of Harken's impending financial doom at least twice during the month he cashed out. Bush himself was never questioned in the investigation. And four times Bush missed federally mandated filing deadlines by more than three months (thus concealing his transactions from average shareholders), though he had an explanation for that: He filed on time; the SEC must have misplaced his paperwork. *Four times.*

Baseball

9. What did George W. Bush say about putting together the deal to buy the Texas Rangers?

A. "Finally, after going to Andover and Yale like my dad did, and getting tapped for Skull & Bones like he did, and learning how to fly like he did, and going into the oil business like he did—even opening up an office in the same building he opened his first office in—and going into politics like he did, I found something I wanted to do that he hadn't already done."

B. "I had pursued the purchase like a pit bull on the pant leg of opportunity."

C. "I never had any doubt that it would work out my way in the end, because I was prepared to do anything to win."

D. "You know, my lifelong dream has been to be commissioner of baseball, so this was just a natural step to take."

ANSWER: B. Though his own $606,000 investment in the team gave him a mere 1.8 percent stake, he was delighted to have the world believe he was "the owner," and to that end he cheer-led at home games—remember, he was a cheerleader at prep school—from the owner's box, and handed out baseball cards with his picture. As he explained to *Time* reporter Laurence I. Barrett in 1989, "My biggest liability in Texas is the question 'What's the boy ever done?' . . . Now I can say, 'I've done something—here it is.'"

10. What would sixty-nine-year-old café/motel owner Maree Fanning say to George W. Bush if the opportunity presented itself?

    A. "Go to hell."
    B. "Speak much?"
    C. "You're a bad, bad man."
    D. "Bite my ass."

ANSWER: D. She and her family had refused to sell her land to Bush and his consortium for their new baseball stadium's parking lot. "If you don't sell it, we're going to condemn it," he told her, and that's just what happened, resulting in her getting paid a fraction of what the land was worth. A lawsuit ultimately led to a settlement that provided the Fannings with proper financial compensation, but still they *hate* Bush.

11. What did the national TV cameras catch George W. Bush doing as he sat behind the Texas Rangers' dugout during pitcher Nolan Ryan's three-hundredth victory?

    A. Chugging a nonalcoholic beer
    B. Shouting obscenities at the umpire
    C. Picking his nose
    D. Reading the Bible

ANSWER: C. The segment can be seen at http://www.gwbush.com /multimedia.shtml

Governor of Texas

12. Upon signing on as communications director for George W. Bush's 1994 campaign for the Texas governorship against incumbent Ann Richards, what was the first crisis Karen Hughes had to deal with?

    A. A Richards TV spot that featured the video of Bush picking his nose.
    B. One of the Deke pledges Bush had branded twenty-seven years ago who came forward to show his scar.
    C. On a dove hunt, with a pack of reporters looking on, Bush unwittingly shot a killdeer, which is a protected species.
    D. A Democrat who claimed to have proof that Bush had fallen off the wagon.

ANSWER: C.

Match the categories with Texas's ranking among all states under Governor George W. Bush.

13. Spending on the environment
14. Delivery of social services
15. Spending on teachers' salaries

    A. Forty-seventh
    B. Forty-ninth
    C. Fiftieth

ANSWER: 13-B, 14-A, 15-C. To be fair, though, Texas under Bush did come in first in number of executions, and Houston came in first among polluted cities.

16. What was George W. Bush's explanation as to why Laura Bush was "the perfect wife for a governor"?

A. She wasn't "trying to butt in and always, you know, compete."
B. She was "a schoolteacher and a librarian, and kids learn from books, so, you know, there's the soccer mom vote right there."
C. She "never smokes in public."
D. She's "not that good a writer so she's not gonna come out with some kind of *Bushie Dearest* exposé."

ANSWER: A.

17. As he signed a bill making it legal, for the first time since the days of the Wild West, for Texans to carry concealed guns, George W. Bush explained, "This is a bill to make Texas a safer place." TRUE OR FALSE?

ANSWER: True. And two years later he made it legal to bring hidden guns into churches, hospitals, and amusement parks, making Texas safer still.

18. Who is Joe Frank Cannon?

A. The Democratic lieutenant governor with whom George W. Bush forged a political alliance.
B. The CEO of the Houston-based Services Corporation International (the world's biggest funeral home operation), which seems to have received special treatment from George W. Bush in a dispute with a state agency over embalming practices.

C. A Texas inmate executed under George W. Bush despite his lawyer having slept through much of his trial.

D. A Texas lawyer who slept through much of his client's capital punishment trial.

ANSWER: D. Bob Bullock was the Democratic lieutenant governor. Robert Waltrip was the funeral home CEO. Carl Johnson was the lackadaisically represented inmate. And Cannon was far from the only lawyer who snoozed during death penalty cases. Another, John E. Benn, explained himself like this: "I'm seventy-two years old. I customarily take a short nap in the afternoon."

19. According to George W. Bush's autobiography, "by far the most profound" decision a governor is faced with is whether to allow an execution to be carried out. "I get the facts, weigh them thoughtfully and carefully, and decide." According to information contained in his daily schedules, how long did he typically devote to this thoughtful and careful weighing?

A. Fifteen minutes, half an hour tops.

B. An hour, maybe an hour and a half.

C. Four or five hours.

D. A difficult case could consume him for days and keep him up nights.

ANSWER: A. In his six years as governor, Texas executed 152 people, an average of one every two weeks—a national gubernatorial record.

20. George W. Bush mortified his teenage daughter Barbara by teasing her about phone calls from her boyfriend while a camera crew was in the governor's

22

mansion filming the decoration of the Christmas tree. TRUE OR FALSE?

ANSWER: False. It was Barbara's twin, Jenna, that he teased.

21. What was George W. Bush's response to an Agriculture Department report which found that 13 percent of Texans are unable to meet their basic food needs and 5 percent actually suffer from hunger?

A. He offered some unparsable sentence fragments about "compassionate conservatism."
B. He said, "Tell 'em to commit some capital crimes and we'll put 'em out of their misery."
C. He claimed to know of no such cases and said, "You'd think the governor would have heard if there are pockets of hunger in Texas," failing to mention that a good reason for his ignorance was that several years earlier he'd vetoed a bill that would have gathered this data.
D. He wept—he actually wept—to hear that another human being was suffering.

ANSWER: C.

22. According to his daily schedules as governor, George W. Bush spent half an hour a day playing video golf or computer solitaire. TRUE OR FALSE?

ANSWER: False. He actually spent more like an hour and a half a day at these pursuits, possibly as a way to relax after his two-hour midday exercise regimen.

23. Who was the first to dub George W. Bush "Shrub"?

A. Jim Reese, in his losing 1978 Republican primary race against him

B. Ann Richards, in her losing 1994 gubernatorial race against him

C. Molly Ivins, in her newspaper columns

D. His mother

ANSWER: A. Richards, who is often erroneously credited with coining the term, nonetheless *was* the first to say, "If his name was Richard Nixon, hey, he wouldn't even be in the running." Ivins was the first to use "Shrub" in the title of a book about Bush. As for Barbara Bush, she hates it when anyone calls him "Dubya," so "Shrub" really wouldn't be her thing.

24. George W. Bush's explanation for his resistance to expanding health insurance coverage (in a state that ranked forty-ninth out of fifty for women and children and fiftieth for families) even though Texas had a record-breaking surplus was that "in times of plenty, the government must not overcommit because we may not have times of plenty in the future." TRUE OR FALSE?

ANSWER: True, though such fears for the future didn't stop him from pushing for a $45 million tax break for the oil and gas industries, or for a $1.8 billion tax cut for the wealthy. As Al Gore said, "If you were governor of the state that ranked dead last, fifty out of fifty in health insurance for families, and all of a sudden you found that you had the biggest surplus in the history of your state, wouldn't it occur to you to use some of that surplus to maybe move up in the rankings on health care for families from fifty to forty-five or forty or even better? That's not what happened there."

25. How did George W. Bush make his fortune?

A. He "hit the big one" with a West Texas oil well.

B. He got a huge advance for his campaign autobiography.

C. Having used various family connections to raise the money to buy the Texas Rangers, and having wheedled $135 million worth of corporate welfare out of the state, which levied a sales tax in order to build a new stadium for the team, he made almost $15 million on his original $606,000 investment when the team was sold.

D. Kickbacks from executioners.

ANSWER: C.

Quiz #4

The Republican Primary

Airhead Apparent

1. What was the title of George W. Bush's campaign autobiography, which was actually mainly written by his aide Karen Hughes?

    A. *Don't Call Me Junior!*
    B. *The Cattleless Hat*
    C. *A Charge to Keep*
    D. *The Jerk Behind the Smirk*

ANSWER: C.

2. The first crisis of George W. Bush's presidential campaign came with his 1999 refusal to say whether or not he'd ever done drugs. At first he tried to paint it as a matter of good parenting, advising other baby boomers to be less than forthright with their own kids—"I think the baby boomer parent ought to say, 'I've learned from mistakes I may or may not have made'"—but ultimately he couldn't avoid answering a reporter's question about whether he could meet the seven-years-drug-free standard that appointees to his administration would have to meet. He could, he said. In fact, he could meet the more stringent fifteen-year standard that applied when his father became president in 1989. In fact, he could have met that standard back then. What can reasonably be assumed from all of this?

A. Anyone who'd never done drugs would have no problem sharing that information with the voting public.
B. Given what we know of his daughters' fondness for alcohol, he might have been better off leveling with them.
C. He must have done a *lot* of blow in 1974.
D. All of the above.

ANSWER: D, and just imagine what a twenty-eight-year-old George W. Bush must have been like on coke. As for "mistakes I may or may not have made," wrote *New York Times* columnist Maureen Dowd, "It's not moral instruction. It's not even wisdom. It's evasion."

3. Senator Robert Bennett (R-Utah) predicted that George W. Bush would be the Republican nominee in 2000 unless "he was hit by a bus or _____"

A. some other large, deadly vehicle.
B. some woman comes forward, let's say some black woman comes forward, with an illegitimate child that he fathered within the last eighteen months.

C. people get sick of his smirk.

D. got caught with a straw up his nose.

ANSWER: B.

4. Asked on an MTV special (about the college days of the candidates) whether he "chose to" smoke pot as a youth, George W. Bush replied wittily, "Well, I don't think anyone *made* you smoke." TRUE OR FALSE?

ANSWER: False. That was Al Gore's response. Bush was the only major candidate to refuse to be interviewed, possibly because his campaign could in no way benefit from an examination of his Yale years.

5. Who is Zack Exley?

A. The Republican ad man who opined that "compassionate conservative" is "a terrific slogan. The word 'compassion' is something that is important in people's lives. You could almost drop 'conservative.' That's how good the word is."

B. The governor who introduced George W. Bush at a presidential campaign rally with this anecdote: "George and I were at one of these governors' conferences, and he turns to me and says, 'What are they talking about?' I said, 'I don't know,' and he said, 'You don't know a thing, do you?' And I said, 'Not one thing,' and he said, 'Neither do I,' and we kind of high-fived."

C. The Boston TV reporter who ambushed George W. Bush by asking him to name the leaders of four countries (Chechnya, India, Pakistan, and Taiwan), to which the obviously pissed-off candidate could only take one lucky guess ("Lee"), thus getting half-credit for Chinese president Lee Teng-hui, and scoring 12.5 percent on the quiz.

D. The creator of gwbush.com, a parody Web site featuring, among other things, doctored photos of Bush snorting cocaine and streaming video (undoctored) of Bush picking his nose at a Rangers game, all of which prompted Bush to say, "There ought to be limits to freedom," a statement that was then put on T-shirts and bumper stickers and sold on the site.

ANSWER: D. Sig Rogich is the slogan fan. Gary Johnson is the governor (of New Mexico). Andy Hiller is the TV reporter whose pop quiz prompted *New York Times* columnist Thomas L. Friedman to write, "What was scary was not that George W. didn't know all the names. It was the Quayle-in-the-headlights look on his face when he was asked for them. If I were the Democrats, I would run commercials over and over again just showing that look on his face. And the voice-over would say, 'Here's how George W. looked when he was asked to name the leaders of Taiwan, India, Pakistan, and Chechnya. Imagine how he would look if he were asked what to do about them.'"

The Debates

6. Determined to prove that he now knew the answers to the world leaders pop quiz he had recently flunked, George W. Bush demanded that a debate moderator ask him for the name of India's president and, when asked, triumphantly crowed, "Vajpayee!" Unfortunately, Vajpayee was India's prime minister, so Bush was wrong again. TRUE OR FALSE?

ANSWER: True. The correct answer to the question Bush had posed to himself was "Narayanan!"

7. What book did George W. Bush claim to be reading, only to be asked about it during a debate and find himself with nothing to say, leading him to protest that it would be impossible to do the book justice "in a minute's time," and then, finally, to come up with the profound "lessons" of the book: "Our nation's greatest export to the world has been, is, and always will be the incredible freedoms we understand in the great land called America"?

> **A.** A collection of Ronald Reagan's speeches
> **B.** A biography of Secretary of State Dean Acheson
> **C.** An expose of liberal bias in the media
> **D.** *Governing for Dummies*

ANSWER: B.

8. What made George W. Bush chuckle during a debate in Los Angeles?

> **A.** He remembered the time candidate Gary Bauer fell off the stage during a pancake-making contest in New Hampshire.
> **B.** Alan Keyes referred to "Greeks" instead of "Grecians."
> **C.** Steve Forbes mentioned one of Bush's favorite scenes from the Austin Powers movie.
> **D.** The moderator talked about how the lawyer for a Texas death row inmate slept through much of the trial.

ANSWER: D.

9. What was George W. Bush's answer when asked at a debate to name his favorite philosopher?

A. "Aquinas, because he was able to combine Aristotelian and neo-Platonist elements of philosophy in a Christian context."

B. "Kant, because he synthesized the rationalism of Leibniz and the skepticism of Hume."

C. "Christ, because he changed my heart."

D. "Neech *(sic)*, because it was all about Superman."

ANSWER: C. Still, his reaction, when asked to elaborate—a patronizing "Well, if they don't know, it's going to be hard to explain"—left at least one viewer thinking that the heart transformation was not yet complete.

The Straight Talk Express

10. The first time George W. Bush and Senator John McCain (R-Ariz.) came face-to-face while campaigning in New Hampshire, Bush walked right up to his rival, planted himself in front of him, and stared pugnaciously with his face mere inches from McCain's, as if to say, "Whuddya gonna do about it?" TRUE OR FALSE?

ANSWER: False. According to *Time* magazine, Bush "draped himself over McCain like a coat" and said, "I love you, man," and McCain's skin "nearly wriggled off in discomfort."

11. When George W. Bush, who was at the time viciously savaging John McCain in the South Carolina primary, took McCain's hands during a break in a debate and appealed to him for less acrimony between them, McCain snarled, "Don't give me that shit, and take your hands off me." TRUE OR FALSE?

ANSWER: True.

12. What did George W. Bush do during the Republican primaries?

A. Falsely implied that John McCain, who spent five and a half years as a Vietnam prisoner of war while Bush himself had managed to evade the draft by using his connections to get into the Texas National Guard, was weak on veterans' issues.
B. Absurdly promoted himself as "somebody who comes from outside the system."
C. Ran a radio spot falsely claiming that John McCain "opposes funding for vital breast cancer programs," and then, after being told that McCain's sister had breast cancer, callously said, "All the more reason to remind him of what he said about the research that goes on here."
D. All of the above.

ANSWER: D.

13. On the day after being soundly trounced by John McCain in the New Hampshire primary, whose endorsement did George W. Bush receive in an effort to turn his campaign around?

A. Bob Dole's
B. Gerald Ford's
C. Nancy Reagan's
D. Dan Quayle's

ANSWER: D.

14. How did George W. Bush reach out to McCain voters after defeating him for the Republican presidential nomination?

A. He told a reporter that McCain "didn't change my views" on campaign finance reform or, for that matter, on anything else.
B. Responding to a reporter's observation that McCain had inspired record voter turnouts in the primaries, he snapped, "Well, then, how come he didn't win?"
C. Asked if there was anything he regretted about the vicious campaign he waged, he shot back, "Like what? Give me an example. What should I regret?"
D. All of the above.

ANSWER: D.

15. What did John McCain do at the joint news conference in which he reluctantly announced his support for George W. Bush's candidacy?

A. He made some perfunctory favorable comments but failed to actually say he endorsed Bush until, pressed by reporters, he mockingly declared, "I endorse Governor Bush" six times in a row, then agreed with a reporter who said the whole thing just seemed like McCain was swallowing a necessary dose of party unity medicine.
B. He apologized again for not having had the guts in the South Carolina primary to take a stand against the state's flying the Confederate flag over the capitol in Columbia, thus indirectly shining a light on Bush's continuing refusal to acknowledge his own gutlessness on the issue.
C. He suggested that a good slogan for Bush's tax cuts would be "Windfalls for the Wealthiest."

D. He broke into a giggle when he said, "Governor Bush is the most qualified person to be president of the United States."

Quiz #5

Bushspeak

1. What did George W. Bush say in an effort to reassure voters that he was up to the job of being president?

A. "I have had foreign policy as the governor of Texas and that is with Mexico, and I've handled it well."
B. "I've been elected governor twice in an incredibly important state."
C. "I understand small business growth. I was one."
D. All of the above.

ANSWER: D.

2. Complete George W. Bush's response to a question about whether or not he'd been spending enough time campaigning in New Hampshire: "The important question is: How many _____"

   A. voters have I convinced?
   B. dollars have I raised?
   C. miles have I run?
   D. hands have I shaked?

ANSWER: D.

3. Three of these statements were made by George W. Bush. Which one did Donald Trump utter before he finished using the pretense of running for president to help promote his latest book?

   A. "If you're sick and tired of the politics of cynicism and polls and principles, come and join this campaign."
   B. "Rarely is the question asked: Is our children learning?"
   C. "I think the only difference between me and the other candidates is that I'm more honest and my women are more beautiful."
   D. "The American people is supportive of me."

ANSWER: C.

4. Whose alleged dirty campaigning did George W. Bush complain about by saying, "He can't take the high horse and then claim the low road"?

   A. John McCain
   B. Lamar Alexander
   C. Alan Keyes
   D. Orrin Hatch

ANSWER: A.

5. Speaking at a New Hampshire school that was featuring, as its theme of the month, "Perseverance," George W. Bush said, "I appreciate perversity in all its forms. It's important if you're running for president. You've got to perverserate." TRUE OR FALSE?

ANSWER: False. Still, he *did* say, "This is preservation month. I appreciate preservation. It's what you do when you run for president. You've got to preserve."

6. Complete George W. Bush's campaign pledge: "If I'm elected president, I'm going to tell all the moms and dads we need to _____ our love for our children."

A. double
B. redouble
C. triple
D. retriple

ANSWER: B.

7. Three of these statements were made by George W. Bush. Which one did his father utter back in the day?

A. "[My wife] and I really don't realize how bright our children is sometimes until we get an objective analysis."
B. "It's no exaggeration to say the undecideds could go one way or the other."
C. "There is madmen in the world and there are terror."
D. "When I was coming up, it was a dangerous world and we knew exactly who the 'they' were. It was us versus them, and it was clear who 'them'

was. Today, we're not so sure who the 'they' are, but
we know they're there."

8. What did George W. Bush say about Internet millionaires?

A. "[They were] in the right time at the right
place."
B. "It's like the revenge of the nerds."
C. "[They've] become rich beyond their means."
D. "Snake oil never goes out of fashion."

9. In a *Newsweek* interview, George W. Bush complained about his father having become "the gist for cartoonists" and said he was none too crazy about "getting pillared in the press" himself. TRUE OR FALSE?

10. Complete George W. Bush's description of his record as governor: "I've got a record, a record that is conservative and a record that is _____"

A. consistified.
B. compassionated.
C. constipated.
D. a grotesque celebration of indifference and
hardheartedness.

11. George W. Bush confused Slovakia with Slovenia and called Greeks "Grecians." How did he refer to those who live in East Timor?

   A. "The East Timorese"
   B. "The East Timorians"
   C. "The East Timoranians"
   D. "The East Timorestrians"

ANSWER: B. The proper way is, of course, A.

12. How did George W. Bush mangle the phrase "the post–Cold War world"?

   A. The "World War Cold"
   B. The "Cold Post War"
   C. The "Prewar World"
   D. The "Post Cold World"

ANSWER: D.

13. George W. Bush used to say he wanted to "incent" people to behave more responsibly, but when informed that this was not a verb, he switched to "incentivate." TRUE OR FALSE?

ANSWER: False. "Incentivize."

14. Complete George W. Bush's declaration of empathy: "I know how hard it is _____"

   A. to feed your family.
   B. to put food on the table.
   C. to fad your foomily . . . to food your feem . . . to eat.
   D. to put food on your family.

ANSWER: D.

15. Complete George W. Bush's statement after his postprimary meeting with John McCain: "I think we agree, _____"

A. the past is over.
B. the future is on its way.
C. the present is stuck between the past and the future.
D. the recent past is more recent than the distant.

Quiz #6

The Critics Speak

1. Complete David Letterman's quote about George W. Bush: "I have the feeling that this guy could turn out to be _____"

   A. an election stealer.
   B. a great president.
   C. a colossal boob.
   D. Lord Voldemort.

ANSWER: C.

2. On what did *The Washington Post*'s Michael Kelly base his prediction, made ten months before the election, that George W. Bush would be the next president?

   A. His sense that "if it's a choice between a frat boy and a policy wonk, look out, wonk. They know Gore is smarter, but Bush is the guy who'll make sure the pizza gets delivered."

B. The popularity at the time of *Who Wants to Be a Millionaire,* "a program rooted in the brilliant premise that stupidity and ignorance need be no impediment in a contest of the intellect."

C. His foresight that Green Party candidate Ralph Nader would turn out to be "the suicide bomber of progressive politics."

D. His belief that voters would "be suckered in by Bush's 'I'm a uniter, not a divider' mantra, and boy, will they be in for a rude awakening."

ANSWER: B. And, sadly, Kelly was right. And Bush started a war that Kelly went off to cover, and he lost his life there.

3. Complete *New York Observer* writer Philip Weiss's observation about George W. Bush: "His father reminded women of their first husband, but George W. reminds them of the guy who _____ them sophomore year."

A. studied with
B. drank beers with
C. protested the war with
D. date-raped

ANSWER: D.

4. What observation appeared in a daily newspaper column about George W. Bush's appearance on David Letterman's show, where the host asked him to explain his campaign slogan, "A uniter, not a divider," and Bush, attempting to be funny about Letterman's recent heart surgery, said bizarrely, "That means when it comes time to sew up your chest cavity, we use stitches as opposed to opening it up. That's what that means"?

A. "This is something that could only have been said by someone who was seriously, deeply, not bright."

B. "How sidesplitting."

C. "You generally find this level of performance on a talk show only when the guest is a troubled actress facing a midlife crisis. . . . [He exhibited] the complete repertoire of his least attractive expressions—the smirk, the nervously darting eyes, that trapped look that always makes Mr. Bush resemble a small mammal in distress."

D. All of the above.

ANSWER: D. The comments are by, respectively, columnists Michael Kelly, Molly Ivins, and Gail Collins.

5. Complete *Washington Post* columnist Richard Cohen's observation about George W. Bush: "Bush is a unique politician. Most of them stand for very little. He stands for _____"

A. integrity.

B. fairness.

C. nothing.

D. revenge.

ANSWER: C.

Who said what about George W. Bush?

6. "You get the feeling with W., as with Sonny [Corleone], that he's one insult away from blowing up and losing his chance at succession. It's there, bristling right beneath the surface, that unforgiving, unforgetting, tart-tongued nature he inherited from his mother."

7. "The suddenly widespread concern about Bush's mastery of substance leaves untouched a question that may be equally important: Is Bush too peevish to be president?"

8. "Frankly, I can't imagine why anyone would consider him for president. He's not smart, he doesn't know much, and he doesn't work hard. The truth is, he is not terribly interested in government or how it works. Damned if I know why he's running."

9. "He has the carriage and energy of a bantam. The effect is marred only by a face that is slightly too small for his head, making it look like an overstuffed softball."

A. *Fort Worth Star Telegram* columnist Molly Ivins.
B. *Washington Post* columnist Marjorie Williams.
C. *New York Times* columnist Maureen Dowd.
D. *New York Observer* columnist Richard Brookhiser.

ANSWER: 6-C, 7-B, 8-A, 9-D.

10. Complete this observation by *New York Times* columnist Gail Collins: "If Dan Quayle looked like a deer caught in the headlights when he was in front of the cameras, Mr. Bush sometimes resembles _____"

A. a proud lion, fiercely defending his positions as if they were his cubs.
B. a salmon struggling to swim upstream.

C. a chimpanzee.

D. a possum cornered in the garage—hunched over, tense, eyes darting worriedly.

ANSWER: D.

Quiz #7

The Race Begins

The Convention

1. According to *New York Times* columnist Maureen Dowd, which dead author would have loved the spectacle of "a millennial convention rooting for the goof-off son of the fired boss to get the big job"?

A. John O'Hara
B. Truman Capote
C. F. Scott Fitzgerald
D. Evelyn Waugh

ANSWER: A. As Dowd wrote, O'Hara, "who savored the self-destructive streak among the pampered, would have enjoyed Bushville as much as Gibbsville."

2. As openly gay Representative Jim Kolbe (R-Ariz.) delivered a speech about international trade, members

46

of which state's delegation bowed their heads in prayer as a sign of protest?

A. Alabama

B. Texas

C. Wyoming

D. Florida

ANSWER: B. And protest against what? That a gay man was allowed to speak (though not about anything related to being gay)? That a gay man was allowed in their party? That a gay man was allowed to breathe air?

3. Complete *New Yorker* writer Joe Klein's observation about George W. Bush accepting his party's nomination in Philadelphia: "He delivered his big speech _____, with his eyebrows tangled up in each other and his smallish features—eyes, nose, mouth—compressed together in the middle of his face."

A. determinedly

B. assuredly

C. enthusiastically

D. fretfully

ANSWER: D.

The Running Mate

4. Complete *New York Times* columnist Maureen Dowd's observation: "Mr. Cheney was picked because he is the anti-Quayle. George I was determined that George II would not repeat his mistake, choosing someone young and callow. _____"

A. No, that wouldn't do at all.

B. Quayle had definitely been a disaster.

C. Gravitas, that's what was needed.

D. The ticket already had that covered.

5. What was Dick Cheney's explanation for failing to vote in fourteen of the sixteen elections that were held between the time he registered in Dallas County and was picked as George W. Bush's running mate?

A. He said, "I traveled a great deal. My focus was on global concerns"—though this hardly explained his failure to procure absentee ballots.

B. He cited "health problems—big-time"—though this hardly explained his failure to procure absentee ballots.

C. He admitted that he was "uncomfortable" in public places where "total strangers can just come up and talk to me"—though this hardly explained his failure to procure absentee ballots.

D. He said his dog ate his absentee ballots.

6. During the 2000 campaign, what did Dick Cheney's wife, Lynne, say "drives me crazy"?

A. "The way Linda Tripp has been ostracized. It's gotten to the point in this country where people can't even recognize a hero when she's staring them in the face."

B. "When Hillary acts like the happy wife. Walking

hand in hand off the helicopter together at critical moments. It's just so distressing to me."

C. "These writers who say things like Dick has 'all the warmth and charm of an armadillo,' or that 'he smiles as if his lips were sewn shut.' I'll read something like that and I'll think, I want that person dead."

D. "Whenever anyone tries to talk to me about Mary [her openly gay daughter]. I mean, part of me feels so silly, you know, saying things like, 'Mary has never declared such a thing' when in fact she's been out for years, she's as out as out can be. But damn it, I just refuse to give it to them, I won't give them the satisfaction. They're always so happy about it, you can tell, they're like, 'Ha ha, look who has a gay daughter: Little Miss Intolerant.' "

ANSWER: B.

7. What song did Lynne Cheney disapprovingly distribute lyrics to while testifying against violence in music and movies in a Senate hearing?

A. Eminem's "Kim"
B. Johnny Cash's "Folsom Prison Blues"
C. Eminem's "Kill You"
D. Warren Zevon's "Excitable Boy"

ANSWER: C.

8. To what was Dick Cheney referring when he said, "There's so much time and energy and effort devoted to this kind of trivia"?

A. The continuing media interest in stories like O. J. Simpson's periodic brushes with the law in Florida and Michael Jackson's bizarre fondness for young boys.

B. Reality TV shows like *Survivor* and *Who Wants to Marry a Millionaire*.

C. *Harry Potter and the Goblet of Fire*.

D. His congressional voting record, which included votes for abolishing the Education Department and defunding the Head Start program, and votes against a ban on "cop killer" armor-piercing bullets, against a ban on plastic guns that can pass through metal detectors, against the Clean Water Act, against the Endangered Species Act, against the Equal Rights Amendment, against a school lunch program, against a congressional resolution calling on South Africa to free Nelson Mandela, and, of course, against federal funding for abortions, even in cases of rape, incest, or when the mother's life was endangered.

ANSWER: D.

9. What did Dick Cheney say when it was revealed that he and his wife, whose income over the previous ten years was over $20 million, had given a meager 1 percent to charity?

A. "And why is this anyone's business but ours?"

B. "That's a choice that individuals have to make, in terms of what they want to do with their resources. It's not a policy question. It's a private matter. It's a matter of private choice."

C. "George and Laura only gave 3 percent. Is that really so much more? Why don't you go bust their chops?"

D. "Okay, you got me. I guess generosity isn't really our thing."

ANSWER: B.

10. Unlike his running mate George W. Bush, Dick Cheney was never arrested for drunk driving as a younger man. TRUE OR FALSE?

ANSWER: False. Unlike his running mate George W. Bush, who was arrested once for drunk driving, young Dick Cheney was arrested twice for this offense.

Quiz #8

The Fall Campaign

On the Trail

1. What did *New York Times* reporter Adam Clymer do to so upset George W. Bush that he referred to him, unaware that there was an open microphone nearby, as a "major league asshole," to which Dick Cheney sycophantically added, "Oh, yeah, he is. Big-time"?

A. He wrote a story about the drinking habits of Bush's teenage daughters.
B. He wrote a story in which he interviewed psychoanalysts about Bush's behavior.
C. He wrote a story about the fatal automobile accident Laura was involved in when she was seventeen.
D. He wrote a story debunking Bush's claims

glorifying the state of health care in Texas, pointing out just how terrible it really was, and then wrote another story exposing the lies in a Bush campaign ad about prescription drugs.

2. How did a friend describe George W. Bush's beliefs about creationism vs. evolution?

A. "I know, I know, you'd think an Ivy League education would set a lad straight about this, but he says he's not sure."
B. "We'd spend hours and hours every weekend debating the relative merits of each."
C. "He thinks that if you believe in evolution God will punish you by tossing you off the edge of the earth."
D. "He doesn't really care about that kind of thing."

3. What did George W. Bush tell voters about the budget surplus he would inherit if he became president?

A. "It's an opportunity to extend health insurance to every single American."
B. "It's burning a hole in my pocket and I'm not even president yet."
C. "It's your money. You paid for it."
D. "You think this surplus is big? Just wait till you see the deficit at the end of my first term. It'll block out the sun."

4. Who is Tom Connolly?

A. The National Rifle Association vice president who said that if George W. Bush is elected, "we'll have a president where we work out of their office."

B. The actor who coached the man who played George W. Bush in Al Gore's practice debates, who observed, "There's always this *fear* in Bush's eyes . . . and there's the smugness he uses to cover it."

C. The former secretary of veterans affairs who questioned Bush's and Cheney's commitment to the military, given that neither volunteered to serve in Vietnam.

D. The Maine lawyer who made sure the secret of George W. Bush's 1976 DUI arrest became known five days before the election, calling the revelation an "act of democracy" and explaining that "It's not a dirty trick to tell the truth."

5. After repeatedly referring to George W. Bush's DUI arrest as an incident from his "youth," what did communications director Karen Hughes say when asked if a thirty-year-old man could really be considered a "youth"?

A. "He can if we say it often enough."

B. "I'll just say this. He was still bringing his dirty laundry to his friends' wives to wash."

C. "It was before he was married. It was before he had children."

D. "Some days I think a fifty-four-year-old could."

The Tube

6. Bush staff members were so delighted with his smoochy-woochy appearance with Oprah Winfrey that they instantly told reporters the campaign was being inundated with favorable calls from viewers across America, though in fact the show had only just finished taping and had not yet actually been seen by people across America. TRUE OR FALSE?

7. What was George W. Bush's response when asked by Oprah what he thought was the public's biggest misperception of him?

    A. "I favor the rich."
    B. "I've got a short fuse."
    C. "I langle the manguage."
    D. "I'm running on my daddy's name."

8. After an anti-Gore TV spot was found to contain a single frame flashing the word "RATS," what kind of intent did George W. Bush deny four times that there had been any of?

A. "Sublime"

B. "Sublinian"

C. "Subliminable"

D. "Subliminial"

ANSWER: C. He had no idea what the actual word meant, as was made obvious by his defense: "There's one frame out of nine hundred. It is difficult—it's impossible to see it, you know, just if you run it and look at it on TV." Or, in a word, subliminal. As *New Republic* writer Jonathan Chiat explained, "Bush didn't know what it meant, only that it must be something bad. And how could his advertisement be subliminable if the offending word only occupied one frame?"

9. What did *Time* columnist Margaret Carlson say about George W. Bush walking onstage on *Live with Regis* monochromatically dressed exactly like host Philbin?

A. "He makes a better Regis than he does a serious candidate."

B. "Thank God Kathie Lee retired, or he might have donned spandex."

C. "If this is going to be his shtick, then I can't wait till he meets with Arafat and wraps a doo-rag around his head."

D. "One can only wonder if he'll sport a prosthetic chin with Leno."

ANSWER: B. "Have we come to the point," she asked, "that appearing likable on *Regis* and *Oprah* is as important as doing well in the debates? Really, how much do we have to like the guy whose job is grappling with international crises?"

Match the comic or comedy writer with his line about George W. Bush.

56

10. "Yes, he said 'subliminable,' but he was probably distracted thinking about executing some criminables."

11. "To kind of even things out [after Al Gore's crowd-pleasing convention smooch with Tipper], George Bush and his wife were seen making out at an execution."

12. "[Texas] executed a guy with an I.Q. of sixty-three. Can you believe it? Bush turning his back on one of his own."

13. "I sincerely hope you cast your vote for George W. Bush. I'm a fifty-three-year-old comedy writer and, to be honest, I don't feel like working that hard anymore."

14. [As Bush]: "I was always around when Dick Cheney and my dad worked together. I'd hear 'em working in the front room when I'd stumble in all high."

   A. David Letterman
   B. Jay Leno
   C. Writer Gerard Mulligan
   D. Jon Stewart
   E. Writer Robert Smigel

ANSWER: 10-D, 11-A, 12-B, 13-C, 14-E.

15. What did George W. Bush do when invited by Jay Leno to share an embarrassing story about himself?

   A. He talked about being caught picking his nose on national television.

B. He talked about drunkenly berating Al Hunt in front of his young son.

C. He talked about drunkenly challenging his father to a fight.

D. He talked about how his brother Marvin "actually urinated in a steam iron one time."

ANSWER: D. Marvin was five at the time. In any event, why this would qualify as a story embarrassing to George W. remains unclear.

16. What did George W. Bush say on ABC's *20/20*?

A. "I'm pretty good about asking myself the own question, then answering it, see?"

B. "I don't feel like I've got all that much too important to say on the kind of big national issues."

C. "Now, by the way, surplus means a little money left over, otherwise it wouldn't be called a surplus."

D. "I don't know whether I'm going to win or not. I think I am. I do know I'm ready for the job. And if not, that's just the way it goes."

ANSWER: B. He said everything else, too, just not on *20/20*.

The Debates

17. Complete this statement by George W. Bush before his first debate with Al Gore: "I view this as a chance _____"

A. to prove once and for all that I have what it takes to lead.

B. for me to clearly articulate my positions and philosophy.

C. to whip that wimp's ass.

D. for people to get an impression of me on a stage debating my opponent.

ANSWER: D. Not that it was a chance he particularly welcomed, given the amount of energy his campaign expended in trying to limit the number of debates and the size of the audiences.

18. What accounted for the widespread perception that George W. Bush "won" the first debate, despite the absence of any corroborating evidence in the transcript?

A. Al Gore annoyed viewers by constantly sighing loudly to communicate his contempt, and by not being able to stop saying "lockbox."

B. Expectations for Bush were so low going in that he would have had to have had an outbreak of Tourette's syndrome to have done worse than expected.

C. The media chose to focus on Gore's stupid exaggerations and innocent errors rather than on Bush's out-and-out lies.

D. All of the above.

ANSWER: D.

19. Three of these events took place during the second debate between Al Gore and George W. Bush. Which occurred during their third debate?

A. Bush said, "I hope our European friends become the peacekeepers in Bosnia," when in fact more than 75 percent of the Bosnian peacekeepers at that moment were already non-American.

B. Regarding how he'd conduct foreign policy, Bush said, "If we're an arrogant nation, they'll view us that way. But if we're a humble nation, they'll respect us as an honorable nation."

C. Discussing discrimination against gays, Bush promised, "I'm going to be respectful for people. I'll tolerate people."

D. With Gore pummeling him about affirmative action, Bush complained to moderator Jim Lehrer that Gore was breaking the rules by questioning him directly.

ANSWER: D. He explained, "If affirmative action means quotas, I'm against it. If affirmative action means what I just described, what I'm for, then I'm for it." He then huffed to Gore, "There are certain rules in this that we all agreed to, but evidently rules don't mean anything." As Molly Ivins wrote, "I think Bush threw that [third] debate. Consciously or subconsciously, the poor man knows that he is not prepared to be president of the United States, and he is desperately trying to signal us to that effect."

20. What did George W. Bush refer to as "an important continent"?

A. Asia
B. Africa
C. Australia
D. Austria

ANSWER: B.

21. Which lies did George W. Bush tell in the course of his three debates with Al Gore?

A. He claimed that in his health care program prescription drugs would be "an integral part of Medicare," when in fact this would be true only under Gore's plan, and he claimed to have "brought Republicans and Democrats together" to pass a Texas patients' rights bill, when in fact he had vetoed such a bill and then reluctantly let another become law without his signature.

B. He claimed that the bulk of his tax cuts would go to "the people at the bottom end of the economic ladder," when in fact the opposite was true, and he claimed that the Gore campaign was outspending the Bush campaign, when in fact the opposite was true—by a margin of $50 million.

C. He claimed that the percentage of Texas kids without health insurance had dropped since he'd been governor, when in fact it had risen, and that the percentage of kids nationally without health insurance had risen during the Clinton-Gore years, when in fact it had dropped.

D. All of the above.

ANSWER: D.

22. Explaining that Texas didn't need new hate crime laws to punish the killers of brutally murdered James Byrd, George W. Bush said with a big smile, "Guess what? The three men who murdered James Byrd, guess what's going to happen to them? They're going to be put to death." TRUE OR FALSE?

ANSWER: True. And guess what? Only two of the three were actually sentenced to death. And guess what else? Lots of people were really creeped out by that smile.

Profiles in . . . Well, Not Courage, Exactly

23. How did George W. Bush distinguish himself in Tucker Carlson's 1999 profile of him in the premiere issue of *Talk* magazine?

A. He had a Nixonian outburst about his rival candidates spreading vicious lies about him.

B. He struggled to think of who his heroes were, only managing to come up with pitcher Nolan Ryan.

C. He made fun of Karla Faye Tucker, a woman whose execution he'd chosen not to delay.

D. All of the above.

ANSWER: D. Damage control efforts included Bush claiming that he hadn't really been interviewed at all, that their conversation had an informal structure and "wasn't a sit-down interview" (though the discussion about Karla Faye Tucker took place during a car ride and so, seemingly, couldn't have been anything but). Carlson described Bush mocking the condemned woman's pleas as he recounted a Larry King interview with her: "He asked her real difficult questions, like 'What would you say to Governor Bush?' " And what was her answer? " 'Please,' Bush whimpers, his lips pursed in mock desperation, 'don't kill me.' " For the record, a transcript shows that the King-Tucker exchange Bush recalled never took place, at least not on television. Said rival presidential hopeful Gary Bauer, "If you are going to call yourself a compassionate conservative, you might want to look up the meaning of compassion."

24. According to Gail Sheehy's preelection profile in *Vanity Fair*, what did George W. Bush say he'd do differently if he could do it over?

A. He wouldn't have spoken at the Christian far right's famously intolerant and bigoted Bob Jones

University, especially after its president "called my daddy 'the devil.'"

B. He wouldn't have commuted Henry Lee Lucas's sentence because "It spoiled my perfect record."

C. He wouldn't have appointed Marshall, Texas, police chief Charles W. Williams as chairman of a state law enforcement commission a year after Williams went on record claiming that blacks didn't mind being called "nigger" fifty years ago ("Back then we had Nigger Charlie and Nigger Sam, Nigger Joe. And we regarded those people with all the respect in the world. That was their name. They didn't mind. It wasn't any big deal then."). And as for the terms "porch monkey" or "black bastard," well, said Williams, "you just have to show me where it's a racial slur."

D. He said, "I can't think of anything I'd do differently."

ANSWER: D.

25. What was the newsmaking nugget in Gail Sheehy's profile of George W. Bush?

A. Bush had polio as a child.

B. Bush had once harbored dreams of becoming a heart surgeon.

C. Bush practices that smirk in front of a mirror for five minutes a day, right after his run and just before video golf.

D. Bush could very well be dyslexic.

ANSWER: D. Of course he denied it, saying dyslexically of Sheehy, "I never interviewed her." Still, Bush's brother Neil is dyslexic, and it does run in families, and it would explain an awful lot of the nonsense he comes out with, like when "viable" or "vital" becomes "vile," or when "resonate" becomes "resignate," or when "balkanize" becomes "vulcanize," or when "handcuffs" becomes "cuff links," or when "commensurate" becomes "commiserate," or when "ascribed" becomes "subscribed," or when tailpipe "emissions" becomes "admissions," or when "integral" becomes "ingritable," or when "obfuscate" becomes "obsfucate" or "obscufate," or when "tariffs and barriers" becomes "terriers and bariffs," or when "tenets" becomes "tenants" (as in "I don't have to accept their tenants"), or when he comes out with stuff like "Reading is the basics for all learning," or "I will have a foreign-handed foreign policy," or "Families is where our nation finds hope, where wings take dream."

Quiz #9

The Florida Fiasco

The Longest Night

1. Complete Al Gore's response to George W. Bush after he reacted badly to Gore's telephoned unconcession: "Well, you don't have to get _____ about it."

A. testy

B. snarky

C. snippy

D. snappish

ANSWER: C. And when Bush pointed out that he knew he'd won because his brother Jeb had told him so, Gore replied, "Let me explain something. Your younger brother is not the ultimate authority on this."

2. Not only was George W. Bush helped by his brother being the governor of Florida, but the decision by Fox

65

News to be the first to call the state, and the election, for him was made by Fox news analyst—and Bush first cousin—John Ellis. TRUE OR FALSE?

Jews for Buchanan

3. Who was the elections supervisor in Palm Beach County who approved the "butterfly ballot" design, thinking that its awkward layout was more than compensated for by the large type that would surely make it easier for the elderly to cast error-free votes?

- **A.** Theresa LePore
- **B.** Carol Roberts
- **C.** Barbara Pariente
- **D.** Nikki Ann Clark

4. Reform Party candidate Patrick Buchanan, who, in the course of his career, has often found himself defending, sympathizing with, or making excuses for Nazis, received almost 2,700 more votes in largely Jewish Palm Beach County than he did in any other county in Florida. TRUE OR FALSE?

ANSWER: True, and therein lies the surreal tragedy: George W. Bush is in the White House—and Dick Cheney is in the vice president's residence—because several thousand elderly Jewish men and women went to the polls to vote for the first national ticket to feature a Jew and voted for the perceived anti-Semite by mistake.

Cruella DeVil

5. Who said, "I do not believe the possibility of affecting the outcome of the election is enough to justify ignoring a statutory deadline"?

A. Judge N. Sanders Sauls
B. Bush lawyer Barry Richard
C. Florida House Speaker Tom Feeney
D. Florida secretary of state (and Florida Bush campaign cochairman) Katherine Harris

ANSWER: D. In other words, since Bush was ahead by a hair at that moment, enforcing an arbitrary deadline was more important than making sure the guy who actually won the election became president.

6. What dead animal was Katherine Harris photographed holding by its tail?

A. A water moccasin
B. A possum
C. An alligator
D. A dalmatian

ANSWER: B. The photo ran in the December 4, 2000, issue of *People*.

7. How did *Washington Post* writer Robin Givhan describe Katherine Harris's makeup?

A. "Her skin had been plastered and powdered to the texture of prewar walls."

B. "She, to be honest, seems to have applied her makeup with a trowel."

C. "One wonders how this Republican woman, who can't even use restraint when she's wielding a mascara wand, will manage to use it and make sound decisions in this game of partisan one-upmanship."

D. All of the above.

ANSWER: D.

Recounting

8. Three of these terms bandied about in the media basically meant the same thing. Which was a different thing?

A. "Dimpled chads"
B. "Pregnant chads"
C. "Hanging chads"
D. "Bulging chads"

ANSWER: C. The other three referred to chads that had not been fully poked through the ballot, whereas "hanging chads" had been poked through but not fully detached.

9. Eleven percent of Florida's voters in November 2000 were black. According to a U.S. Commission on Civil Rights report, what percent of the ballots rejected were cast by blacks?

A. 11 percent
B. 26 percent

C. 54 percent
D. 63 percent

ANSWER: C.

10. How did George W. Bush describe his recount adviser James A. Baker III?

A. "The guy who cost us the '92 election by waiting too long to take over the campaign, so guess what? He's gonna get us this one, or else."
B. "The person in charge of explaining our position as to why we don't think there needs to be three elections."
C. "The kind of man you'd rather have on your side than . . . than whoever they have on their side."
D. "A guy who probably never thought in a million years *he'd* be workin' for *me*."

ANSWER: B.

11. Confronted on *Meet the Press* by Tim Russert's accusation that the Gore team was trying to invalidate military absentee ballots on "technicalities," who ambushed his own side by caving and advocating giving "the benefit of the doubt to ballots coming in from military personnel"?

A. Gore campaign chairman William Daley
B. Gore running mate Joseph Lieberman
C. Gore adviser Warren Christopher
D. Gore lawyer Ron Klain

And Lieberman wonders why Gore didn't endorse him in 2004.
of course if Gore was ahead the count would never have been frozen,
counted, to have put Gore in front when the count was frozen, though
might otherwise have been legally disqualified—enough votes, if not
dreds of overseas ballots, the large majority of them for Bush, that
ANSWER: B. This stance opened the doors for the counting of hun-

12. In which county was the recount shut down by a violent mob of angry Republicans?

A. Volusia

B. Miami-Dade

C. Broward

D. Nassau

ANSWER: B.

13. Who told Al Gore, "We were just given a new tally this morning, that if we counted all of the votes that have already been counted in some of the recount, we'd actually be ahead by maybe nine votes"?

A. Lawyer David Boies

B. Senator Tom Daschle

C. Lawyer Laurence Tribe

D. Democratic Party chairman Ed Rendell

ANSWER: B.

In Case You Were Wondering What O.J. Made of All This

14. What bit part did O. J. Simpson play in the recount story?

A. His coked-out girlfriend thought she might have voted for the wrong guy.

B. He claimed to know people who sold coke to George W. Bush.

C. He bought coke the night before the election from a guy who then wasn't allowed to vote because he was a convicted felon.

D. As the nation watched the motorcade of ballot-bearing trucks heading north on I-95, an enterprising reporter sought him out to inquire how he thought this one compared with his own San Diego Freeway spectacle. "This is boring!" he declared. "All I could think of was now I know what people went through when they were trying to watch the basketball game and my Bronco was going up the freeway. In my case it may have been a little more intriguing because people didn't know what was going to happen. Here, they know the ballots are going to get to Tallahassee."

ANSWER: **D.** And how's that search for the real killers going? The reporter didn't ask.

Stressing Out

15. How did George W. Bush initially react to the stress of the undecided election?

A. He dove headfirst off the wagon.

B. He had a heart attack.

C. A huge boil erupted above his right cheek.

D. He became so enraged that he actually began biting people.

16. How did an unnamed friend describe George W. Bush's reaction to the ongoing election confusion?

A. "He's spending about fourteen hours a day exercising."
B. "All he can talk about is what he's going to do to Jeb if he loses."
C. "More than anything, he's uncomfortable. He doesn't like the mess."
D. "You saw. He's growing boils."

Bad Judgment

17. When Supreme Court Justice William Rehnquist ordered the recount halted for the last time, he said that continuing the count could cause "irreparable harm" to George W. Bush "by casting a cloud upon what he claims to be the legitimacy of his election." TRUE OR FALSE?

ANSWER: False. It was Antonin Scalia who posited this preposterous theory that it was the job of the Supreme Court to decide who it wanted to win, and then to help protect "the winner" from possible future criticism that, hey, maybe he didn't really win. Though, to be sure, it's hard to see how this would be accomplished by leaving the actual vote count a mystery. As Justice John Paul Stevens wrote, "Counting every legally cast vote cannot constitute irreparable harm." A case could be made that by voting 5–4 along clearly partisan lines to halt the recount, the main irreparable harm was done by the Court to itself.

Postmortem

18. According to a subsequent exhaustive ballot analysis commissioned by eight major news organizations, if the rules for counting ballots signed into Texas law by Governor George W. Bush in 1996 were applied, Bush would have won Florida by six votes. TRUE OR FALSE?

ANSWER: False. Under the rules Bush thought were good enough for his state, Al Gore won by forty-two votes.

19. In a special *Los Angeles Times* Sunday supplement recapping the five weeks of the recount, which company had the section's only advertisement, on the back page?

A. Benetton
B. Gap
C. Halliburton
D. Banana Republic

ANSWER: D. The irony went unremarked upon.

Ralph's Nadir

20. Though Ralph Nader is blamed by millions of people for costing Al Gore Florida, and therefore the presidency, he had actually stayed out of Florida for the last two weeks of the campaign with the specific purpose of giving Gore a clean shot in a close and crucial state. TRUE OR FALSE?

ANSWER: False. He campaigned in Miami three days before the election, actually heating up his anti-Gore rhetoric, calling him "a bully to the powerless and a coward to the powerful," which is so clearly a description of George W. Bush that one can only conclude that Nader actually can't tell the difference. As *Washington Post* writer Dana Milbank wrote of Nader's premise that Democrats and Republicans are basically the same, "This is true if you stand far enough away from the two parties—in the same way New York and Tokyo would look similar if you were standing on the moon."

Quiz #10

The Shortened Transition

Man Here Says He's the President

1. Complete George W. Bush's declaration to the National Republican Committee: "I want everybody to hear loud and clear that I'm going to be the president _____"

A. even though in my whole life I've been to almost no foreign countries.

B. who takes everyone down with me.

C. for a good long time so y'all might as well get used to having a nasty little prick there.

D. of everybody.

ANSWER: **D.** "Whether they voted for me or not," he added, "I'm their president."

2. How did newly appointed American president George W. Bush describe newly elected Mexican president Vicente Fox?

   A. *"Mi amiga."*
   B. "A world leader like myself."
   C. "My border buddy."
   D. "He's a man I know from Mexico."

ANSWER: D.

Cabinet Fever

3. What was the singular feature of virtually all photographs of George W. Bush posing with his cabinet selections?

   A. Everyone was wearing AIDS ribbons.
   B. There clearly exuded from Bush a powerful aura of authority.
   C. Bush stood behind each of them, looking very small and out of focus, and as if he was smelling something bad.
   D. All of the nominees posed next to Bush wearing "I'm with Stupid" T-shirts.

ANSWER: C.

4. Asked if there were any questions he wished he'd asked the embattled Linda Chavez before nominating her as secretary of labor, George W. Bush said, "Yeah, I wish I'd asked her if she ever harbored any illegal aliens." TRUE OR FALSE?

ANSWER: False. What he actually said was, "I would have to ask the questioner. I haven't had a chance to ask the questioners the question they've been questioning." Nonetheless, the controversy was clearly going to sink the nomination and Chavez withdrew her name.

5. About which of his cabinet nominees did George W. Bush say, "From what I've read in the press accounts, she's perfectly qualified"?

    A. Environmental Protection Agency
administrator–designate Christie Todd Whitman
    B. Agriculture Secretary–designate Ann Veneman
    C. Labor Secretary–designate Linda Chavez
    D. Interior Secretary Gale Norton

ANSWER: C. Well, at least he was engaged enough to read about her in the papers.

6. How did Spencer Abraham, George W. Bush's nominee for secretary of energy, distinguish himself while serving as a senator from Michigan?

    A. He introduced a resolution condemning Detroit's own Eminem.
    B. He voted against every measure that sought to curb automobile pollution.
    C. He was one of three senators who introduced legislation to abolish the Department of Energy.
    D. He wrote Bill Clinton a letter apologizing for the "lunatics" in his party.

ANSWER: C.

7. Complete George W. Bush's announcement of his appointment of Mel Martinez as secretary of housing and

urban development: "I also have picked a secretary for
_____"

A. Health and Human Services.

B. Housing and Human Development.

C. the Housing Humans Department.

D. Suburban Housing Construction.

ANSWER: B.

8. Who suggested John Ashcroft for attorney general back in 1988?

A. Jimmy Swaggart

B. Jerry Falwell

C. Pat Robertson

D. Bob Jones

ANSWER: C. He said Ashcroft "would make a superb attorney general . . . just to give you the type of person I'd like to see."

9. "It's said that we shouldn't legislate morality. Well, I think *all* we should legislate is morality." Who said it?

A. Karl Rove

B. John Ashcroft

C. Lynne Cheney

D. William Bennett

ANSWER: B.

10. Ten years before she was nominated to be George W. Bush's secretary of the interior, Gale Norton gave a speech in which she said that there were certain situations where property owners had the "right to pollute." TRUE OR FALSE?

ANSWER: True.

That's Entertainment

11. What pop star did George W. Bush get on stage and "dance" next to at a pre-inaugural event?

A. Justin Timberlake
B. Ricky Martin
C. James Brown
D. Wayne Newton

ANSWER: B. Remember him?

12. Who actually followed through on his threat to leave the country if George W. Bush became president?

A. Pierre Salinger
B. Robert Altman
C. Eddie Vedder
D. Alec Baldwin

ANSWER: A.

The Oratorically Challenged

13. George W. Bush said three of these things during his transition. Which of them was spoken by Dan Quayle during his transition in 1988?

A. "The person who runs FEMA [Federal Emergency Management Agency] . . . is the first voice oftentimes that someone whose lives have been turned upside down hears from."
B. "We have struggled to not proceed, but to precede to the future of a nation's child."

C. "I know there is a lot of ambition in Washington, obviously. But I hope the ambitious realize they are more likely to succeed with success as opposed to failure."

D. "Verbosity leads to unclear, inarticulate things."

ANSWER: D.

14. Complete George W. Bush's quote: "I believe the results of focusing our attention and energy on teaching children to read and achieving an education system that's responsive to the child and to the parents, as opposed to mired in a system that refuses to change, will make America what we want it to be—a more literate and a _____ country."

A. more wise
B. hopefuller
C. faithfuller
D. more optimum

ANSWER: B.

15. Given the vast liberties he takes with the English language, it's amazing that George W. Bush says the frequently mispronounced word "nuclear" correctly. TRUE OR FALSE?

ANSWER: False. He says "nu-cu-lar."

Quiz #11

Bushspeak

1. Three of these sentences were spoken by George W. Bush. Which one is a classic Quaylism from 1989?

A. "If we do not succeed, then we run the risk of failure."
B. "I am a person who recognizes the fallacy of humans."
C. "A leadership is someone who brings people together."
D. "It's important for us to explain to our nation that life is important."

ANSWER: A.

2. Complete George W. Bush's assessment of Al Gore's tax plan: "It's so prescriptive, it's going to require _____ to even try to figure out what he means."

A. a flying leap of faith
B. one of those big glass future-seeing balls
C. numerous IRS agents
D. numerous IRA agents

ANSWER: D.

3. Three of these statements were uttered by George W. Bush. Which one was spoken long ago by his father?

A. "Insurance—that's a Washington term."
B. "Our priorities is our faith."
C. "[Privatizing] frightens some in Washington, because they want the federal government controlling Social Security, like it's some kind of federal program."
D. "I just am not one who . . . who flamboyantly believes in throwing a lot of words around."

ANSWER: D.

4. George W. Bush made three of these pronouncements on the campaign trail. Which one is a Quayle declaration from 1988?

A. "I know the human being and fish can coexist peacefully."
B. "A tax cut is really one of the anecdotes to coming out of an economic illness."
C. "This election is about who's going to be the next president of the United States."
D. "We'll let our friends be the peacekeepers and the great country called America will be the pacemakers."

ANSWER: C.

5. How important did George W. Bush say that farmers would be to his administration?

A. "Very important. You know, I have a ranch, and that's kind of like a farm."
B. "They will be in the forethought of our thinking."
C. "They are as important as eating is, because they make the food."
D. "Their votes will be seeked very seriously."

ANSWER: B.

6. Three of these statements were uttered by George W. Bush. Which one was spoken long ago by his father?

A. "More and more of our imports come from overseas."
B. "If you say you're going to do something and don't do it, that's trustworthiness."
C. "I will never apologize for the United States of America, ever. I don't care what the facts are."
D. "Expectations rise above that which is expected."

ANSWER: C.

7. George W. Bush made three of these statements during his campaign. Which one was uttered long ago by his father?

A. "I want each and every American to know for certain that I'm responsible for the decisions I make, and each of you are as well."
B. "I'm not the most articulate emotionalist."
C. "They misunderestimated me."

D. "Quotas are bad for America. It's not the way America is all about."

ANSWER: B.

8. Three of these statements were uttered by George W. Bush. Which one is a classic Quaylism from 1988?

A. "The government is not the surplus's money."
B. "The real question . . . is whether we're going to go forward to tomorrow or past to the . . . to the back!"
C. "The legislature's job is to write law. It's the executive branch's job to interpret law."
D. "We cannot let terrorists and rogue nations hold this nation hostile or hold our allies hostile."

ANSWER: B.

9. Complete George W. Bush's statement: "The key to foreign policy is _____"

A. to show no fear.
B. to rely on our allies.
C. to rely on reliance.
D. to defy with defiance.

ANSWER: C.

10. Three of these statements were uttered by George W. Bush. Which one is a classic Quaylism from 1988?

A. "I've supported the administration in Colombia. I think it's important for us to be training Colombians in that part of the world. The hemisphere is in our interest to have a peaceful Colombia."

B. "Natural gas is hemispheric. I like to call it hemispheric in nature because it is a product that we can find in our neighborhoods."

C. "I hope there's some respect and dignity for things I did not do."

D. "Anyway, I'm so thankful and so gracious. I'm gracious that my brother Jeb is concerned about the hemisphere as well."

ANSWER: C.

Quiz #12

The Critics Speak

Who wrote what about George W. Bush?

1. "If George W. Bush isn't a moron, he is a man of impressive intellectual dishonesty and/or confusion. His utterances frequently make no sense in their own terms. His policy recommendations are often internally inconsistent and mutually contradictory. Because it's harder to explain and prove, intellectual dishonesty doesn't get the attention that petty fibbing does, even though intellectual dishonesty indicts both a candidate's character and his policy positions. All politicians, including Al Gore, get away with more of it than they should. But George W. gets away with an extraordinary amount of it."

2. "Jeb has got to feel as if the movie somehow got its reels mixed. He was always the serious son, the focus of the family's political hopes. Now it's as if Jimmy Carter woke up one morning and found they'd nominated Billy."

3. "Nature very often compensates the dyslexic with a higher IQ or some grant of intuitive intelligence. If this is true for Bush it hasn't yet become obvious . . . he has only the downside of his difficulty, which is attention deficit disorder. In the high noon of the age of information, the Republican Party packages and presents a provincial ignoramus who can neither read nor write."

    A. *Nation* columnist Christopher Hitchens
    B. *New York Times* columnist Gail Collins
    C. *Slate* columnist Michael Kinsley

ANSWERS: 1-C, 2-B, 3-A.

4. Complete this quote by Ron Reagan: "The big elephant sitting in the corner is that George W. Bush is simply unqualified for the job. He's probably the least qualified person ever to be nominated by a major party. Yes, he was elected governor of Texas, and before that he ran a baseball team and lost a lot of other people's money in the oil business. But what has happened in the intervening five years to make people believe he'd be a good president? What is his accomplishment? _____ "

    A. That he says 'subliminal' with only one extra syllable?
    B. That he managed to stonewall the media on the coke thing?

C. That he's promised not to giggle or smirk next time he's asked about people he's executed?

D. That he's no longer an obnoxious drunk?

Who wrote what about George W. Bush?

5. "George W. Bush's characteristic approach to a question is to lunge obligingly into it, like a retriever chasing a stick into a pond. Then, after he drops his answer at the questioner's feet, he has nowhere else to go; he restates what he already said, usually less coherently—the way the dog will pick up the stick and drop it again, pick it up, drop it again, until his owner finally makes another throw."

6. "Whatever the opposite of battle-tested is, that's George W. Bush. (Brave fraternity pranks don't count.)"

7. "Mr. Gore is locked into the Good Son role, while Mr. Bush is the Prodigal Son. The Good Son, on his dogged climb to success, can seem like a sycophant. The Prodigal Son, on his circuitous quest, putting his sins behind him, surprising the father who had not expected much, can seem more appealing. What could be more naughty, after all, than running for president when you are aggressively refusing to prepare to assume that office? That is the brazen act of a true rapscallion."

A. *New York Times* columnist Frank Rich
B. *Washington Post* columnist Marjorie Williams
C. *New York Times* columnist Maureen Dowd

8. Complete *L.A. Weekly* columnist Harold Meyerson's observation about George W. Bush's November 26 declaration of victory: "I can't recall a speech in which a presidential hopeful looked more miserable. . . . W. is doubtless aware that he needs to sound conciliatory, visionary, and purposeful all at once during the coming weeks, a daunting task made more so by the fact that _____"

   A. the country's just been through the wringer.
   B. he's got so much to do in so little time.
   C. coherence is not his strong suit.
   D. he is in reality none of these things.

ANSWER: D.

9. Complete *New York Times* columnist Maureen Dowd's observation about George W. Bush's November 26 declaration of victory: "When he comes out to face the cameras he blinks and shrinks, looking tremulous and frightened, dwarfed by American flags. He struggles to exude authority. He furrows his brow, trying to look more sagacious, but he ends up looking as if he has indigestion. Appearing confused at his own speech, he seems _____"

   A. like he wants nothing more than to have a good cry.
   B. like a first-grade actor in a production of *James and the Giant Peach*.
   C. as clueless as a child behind the controls of a 747.
   D. to be wondering what on earth ever made him think he could do this.

ANSWER: B.

10. Which newspaper columnist's sense of outrage compelled him to write column after column proposing a do-over in Florida?

- **A.** *The Washington Post*'s David Broder
- **B.** The New York *Daily News*'s Lars-Erik Nelson
- **C.** *The New York Times*'s William Safire
- **D.** *The New York Times*'s Paul Krugman

ANSWER: B. "It is inconceivable, even intolerable, that one correctable mistake in one county should determine control, against the public will, of both the White House and the Senate," Nelson wrote. "We are entrusting two major branches of government in the greatest power on Earth to the losing party because of a fluke. If we could somehow divine the true votes of Floridians—including those whose ballots were discarded—we would no doubt find that Bush lost the popular vote there, too, but still wins their electoral votes." It was all too much for Nelson, really. Twelve days into the recount drama, he died at home of a stroke, thus sparing himself from ever having to write the phrase "President George W. Bush."

The First Hundred Days

The First Month

1. What did George W. Bush do on his first full day of work in the Oval Office?

    A. He cut off U.S. aid to international family planning groups that counsel women about abortion.
    B. He announced that he was reneging on his campaign pledge to seek reductions in carbon dioxide emissions.
    C. He suspended the ban on building new logging roads in the national forests.
    D. He bombed Iraq.

ANSWER: A. And the irony is that, by cutting off this money, the true effect is to deny women information about nonabortion methods of birth control, resulting in more pregnancies and more abortions. He did B, C, and D, too—just not on his first day.

2. Shortly before noon on a Wednesday in February, disgruntled IRS worker Robert Pickett fired a handgun outside the White House. Dick Cheney was in his office working at the time. Where was George W. Bush and what was he doing?

A. In the Oval Office, pondering how to bring the benefits of his state's health care system—Texas ranked fiftieth in families with health insurance, forty-ninth in women and children insured—to the whole of America.

B. In the Cabinet room with Treasury Secretary Paul O'Neill and economic adviser Lawrence Lindsey debating how best to give the biggest possible chunk of the surplus directly to the wealthy.

C. In the study, running some new nicknames by Karen Hughes.

D. In the residence, working out.

ANSWER: D. One could hardly expect him to stop taking long midday exercise breaks just because he was the president of a whole country now and not just the governor of a really big state.

3. Which former First Lady was reported to refer to George W. Bush as "the village idiot"?

A. Rosalynn Carter
B. Nancy Reagan
C. Hillary Clinton
D. Barbara Bush

ANSWER: B. She denied it, but no sentient human is on record as
believing her.

4. At his first White House news conference, what did
George W. Bush say we needed to do a better job of
helping Colombia to eradicate?

   A. "Coca-Cola"
   B. "Coca leaves"
   C. "Cocoa leaves"
   D. "Coffee leaves"

ANSWER: C.

Bush's Boys

5. Who did George W. Bush describe as "a good man, an
honorable man"?

   A. Donald Rumsfeld
   B. Colin Powell
   C. John McCain
   D. John Ashcroft

ANSWER: A. Powell was described as "a good friend and a good
man," McCain was described as "a good man and a fighter," and
Ashcroft? "A good man. He's got a good heart."

6. Which of George W. Bush's appointees referred to
"the government, whatever that is"?

   A. Treasury Secretary Paul O'Neill
   B. Chief of staff Andrew Card
   C. Attorney General John Ashcroft
   D. Commerce Secretary Don Evans

ANSWER: A.

7. At the midway point of George W. Bush's first hundred days, according to a *New York Times*/CBS News poll, a full 30 percent of Americans believed that people other than Bush are "really running the government most of the time." TRUE OR FALSE?

ANSWER: False. A full 50 percent believed it.

8. Instead of going to a hospital after feeling pain in his chest while exercising, heart attack veteran Dick Cheney went to a birthday party, and then, the next day, after doing two morning TV interviews and then feeling more chest pain, he went to another birthday party, and then, the next day, after feeling still more chest pain in the morning and even more in the afternoon, instead of going to another birthday party, he went to the hospital and had a surgical procedure to reopen an artery in his heart. TRUE OR FALSE?

ANSWER: True.

Getting Down to Business

9. After a U.S. spy plane landed on Chinese soil, what did George W. Bush, whose aides took pains to point out how involved he was in resolving the crisis, say he wanted the crew returned to America "without a lot of"?

    A. "dilly-dallying"
    B. "jabber-jawing"
    C. "diplo-babble"
    D. "hoop-de-la"

ANSWER: D. And the examples provided of Bush's involvement included such laserlike inquiries about the captured crew as "How's their health?" and "Are they getting any exercise?"

10. Complete George W. Bush's thought: "The role of government is to create an environment that encourages Hispanic-owned businesses, women-owned businesses, _____ businesses."

    A. black-owned
    B. Oriental-owned
    C. owner-owned
    D. anybody-kind-of-owned

ANSWER: D.

Headlines

11. Which headline *did not* appear in a daily U.S. newspaper during George W. Bush's first hundred days?

    A. "White House Ends Bar Association Role in Screening Federal Judges"
    B. "Bush Budget on Health Care Would Cut Aid to Uninsured"
    C. "Bush's Budget Would Cut 3 Programs to Aid Children"
    D. "Bush Sees Need for Humility; Says 'After All, I Didn't Really Even Win' "

ANSWER: D.

12. Which headline *did not* appear in a daily U.S. newspaper during George W. Bush's first hundred days?

A. "U.S. Proposes End to Testing for Salmonella in School Beef"
B. "EPA to Abandon New Arsenic Limits for Water Supply"
C. "Moratorium Asked on Suits That Seek to Protect Species"
D. "Bush Acknowledges He Has to Work Harder, Know More"

ANSWER: D.

13. Which headline *did* appear in a daily U.S. newspaper during George W. Bush's first hundred days?

A. "Bush Says Solving Global Warming Problem Is 'Urgent'; Apologizes for Prior Lack of Concern"
B. "She and Bush 'See Eye to Eye on Nothing,' EPA Chief Whitman Says"
C. "Media Declares Bush Legitimacy Off Limits as a Story"
D. "Bush Halts Protection Order for Habitat of Endangered Sheep"

ANSWER: D. He even had it in for the sheep.

The Winter of Some Folks' Discontent

14. Who is Glenn Given?

A. The college student who attracted Secret Service attention by writing an editorial in the school paper urging Jesus Christ to "smite George W. Bush."

B. The Iowa Republican who said of George W. Bush, "There's a certain consistency in the guy's message that tells me he has thought for a long time about his vision for America and how to accomplish it."

C. The aide who was scolded by George W. Bush when a journalist's cell phone rang during a White House photo op with Ariel Sharon.

D. The Pennsylvania Democrat who noted that George W. Bush became visibly annoyed when asked to discuss his positions in any detail, saying, "It's like he wants to say the least he can to get by."

ANSWER: A. Senator Charles Grassley (R-Iowa) is the man so impressed by Bush's vision; Gordon Johndroe was the famously berated aide, and the Pennsylvania Democrat was not speaking for attribution.

15. George W. Bush is the first White House resident to _____

A. trash the environment.

B. blur the lines separating church and state.

C. try to pass off a huge tax windfall for the rich as a boon to the middle class.

D. be the subject of a Web site juxtaposing photographs of him with photos of scarily similar facial expressions on the mugs of chimps.

ANSWER: D. www.bushorchimp.com.

Quiz #14

The Second Hundred Days

Lessons

1. Who is Mia Lawrence?

A. The Yale faculty member—one of the more than two hundred who signed a petition protesting the university's presenting George W. Bush with an honorary doctor of laws degree—who said of Bush, "He's still such a cipher."
B. The Vermont social studies teacher whose honoring at the White House as National Teacher of the Year then-still-Republican Senator James Jeffords was pointedly not invited to, as punishment for his only supporting a $1.35 trillion tax cut as opposed to Bush's preferred $1.6 trillion tax cut.

C. The General Accounting Office manager who said that accounts by Bush aides of significant vandalism done by departing Clinton aides were, by and large, untrue.

D. The Austin bar manager who called the police to tell them that Jenna Bush was trying to buy a margarita with a fake ID.

ANSWER: D. Peter Brooks is the disdainful professor. Michelle Forman, a social studies teacher at Middlebury Union High School, was the vehicle for the White House snub of Jeffords, who soon left the Republican Party, giving control of the Senate to the Democrats. Bernard Unger debunked the vandalism stories. As for Mia Lawrence, it was reported that she turned Jenna in because, well, she hated Jenna's dad.

2. "He has to learn from this, and not just bring people down and feed them cookies, but engage people on some real issues. That means he is going to have to engage himself, educate himself." Which Republican senator said this of George W. Bush after James Jeffords's party switch?

A. Nebraska's Chuck Hagel
B. Rhode Island's Lincoln Chafee
C. Arizona's John McCain
D. Maine's Olympia Snowe

ANSWER: A.

3. Complete this excerpt from George W. Bush's speech at Yale's three hundredth commencement: "To those of you who received honors, awards, and distinctions, I say, 'Well done.' And to the C students, I say, _____"

A. party on!
B. isn't it about time to grow up?

C. make fun of your betters.

D. you, too, can be president of the United States.

ANSWER: D. As Michael Kinsley wrote, "There's a real smugness underlying the self-deprecation: Hey, I'm mediocre and I'm president anyway. . . . Sure, a C student can become president. It helps if his father was president first and his grandfather was a senator and he was born into a family that straddles the Northeast WASP aristocracy and the Sunbelt business establishment."

Headlines

4. Which headline *did not* appear in a daily U.S. newspaper during George W. Bush's second hundred days?

A. "Pushing His Missile Plan in Spain, Bush Calls Arms Treaty a 'Relic.'"

B. "Ashcroft Set to Limit U.S. Holding of Gun Data"

C. "Bush Admits He Hates Crawford Ranch; Keeps It Because Reporters Hate It More"

D. "178 Nations Reach a Climate Accord; U.S. Only Looks On"

ANSWER: C.

5. Which headline *did not* appear in a daily U.S. newspaper during George W. Bush's second hundred days?

A. "White House Wants to Bury Pact Banning Tests of Nuclear Arms"

B. "U.S. Rejects Pact to Enforce Biological Arms Ban"

C. "U.S. Warns It May Skip Conference on Racism"

D. "Bush Finds Error in Fermilab Calculations"

ANSWER: D. It appeared in the humor weekly *The Onion*.

Who? How? What?

6. Who is J. H. Hatfield?

A. The political cartoonist who said of George W. Bush, "It's hard for me not to hear the call of the chimp in those features."
B. The columnist who wrote about George W. Bush, "He is determined to squander the unique opportunity the presidency provides—the opportunity to call us to a cause greater than a $300 rebate."
C. The suicide-committing author of *Fortunate Son,* a book that claimed (unfortunately, with no evidence) that George W. Bush was busted for coke in Texas in the '70s but his dad got him off.
D. The reporter who said to George W. Bush in Madrid, "You say the scientific evidence isn't strong enough to go forward with Kyoto. So, then, how do you justify your missile defense plan when there is even less scientific evidence that that will work?"

ANSWER: C. Steven Brodner is the cartoonist who thinks Bush is chimpish. Arianna Huffington is the columnist. The skeptical reporter wasn't named in the press conference transcript, but since he asked a really pointed question, one can assume he was a member of the foreign press.

7. Who said, "Conservation may be a sign of personal virtue, but it is not a sufficient basis—all by itself—for a sound, comprehensive energy policy"?

A. Secretary of the Interior Gale Norton
B. Dick Cheney

C. White House aide Karl Rove
D. EPA chief Christie Whitman

ANSWER: B.

8. How does Nancy Reagan refer to George W. Bush?

A. "Little George"
B. "Curious George"
C. "Spurious George"
D. "Furious George"

ANSWER: A. When she's not calling him the "Village Idiot," that is.

9. After meeting with the Dalai Lama, what nickname did George W. Bush come up with for him?

A. "Exile Man"
B. "Dolly Parton"
C. None leaked out, though you can be sure a guy who dresses like the Dalai Lama didn't escape the meeting nicknameless.
D. "Tony Lama"

ANSWER: C.

Nice to Meet You

10. What did George W. Bush do when Philadelphia writer Bill Hangley shook his hand at a Fourth of July block party and said, "Mr. President, I hope you only serve four years. I'm very disappointed in your work so far"?

A. He grabbed his hand away and said, "Let me disappoint you a little more. I'm going to steal the next election, too."
B. He turned to a reporter he knew and said, "What a set of *cojones* on this guy!"
C. He smiled genially and said, "You're entitled to your opinion, and that's what's great about this country."
D. He snarled back, "Who cares what you think?"

ANSWER: D.

Hoax

11. In a hoax e-mail that swept the Internet, what did a study conducted by the (nonexistent) Lovenstein Institute of Scranton, Pennsylvania, purport to show?

A. That presidents named Bush tend to be one-termers.
B. That among the last twelve presidents, George W. Bush's IQ was the lowest.
C. That presidents whose only children are two daughters do not serve two full terms.
D. That presidents who have trouble speaking in complete sentences inevitably become the butt of cruel jokes on late-night talk shows.

ANSWER: B. The fake study pegged the IQ at 91, and who knows? Maybe that part is true.

Set Asides

12. Which of these really happened?

A. Treasury Secretary Paul O'Neill said, "If you set aside Three Mile Island and Chernobyl, the safety record of nuclear is really very good."

B. U.S. Surgeon General David Satcher said, "If you set aside the heart disease and the cancer, smoking cigarettes isn't that risky."

C. Attorney General John Ashcroft said, "If you set aside the possibility of erroneous convictions and the statistics that show it having no effect as a deterrent, the death penalty really works."

D. Vice President Dick Cheney said, "Since we set aside the Gore voters who punched his chad and also wrote him in, or who mistakenly punched Buchanan's chad and then wrote in Gore, and we set aside the minority voters and alleged felons who would have voted for Gore if they hadn't been illegally deprived of their right to vote, Bush won Florida big-time."

ANSWER: A.

Quiz #15

The Third Hundred Days

Before

1. Who told NBC's Tim Russert that George W. Bush "read documents, I mean, very thick documents, about the stem cell issue"?

  A. Chief of staff Andrew Card
  B. Press secretary Ari Fleischer
  C. Surgeon General David Hatcher
  D. White House aide Karl Rove

ANSWER: A.

2. What kind of expert did George W. Bush say was coming to his ranch to identify the different types of trees?

  A. "An arborist"
  B. "An arbolist"

C. "An arbonist"

D. "An arsonist"

The Two Hundred Thirty-fifth Day

3. A few months after September 11, George W. Bush shared his memories of that morning with a town meeting in Orlando, Florida: "You're not going to believe what state I was in when I heard about the terrorist attack. I was in Florida. And my chief of staff, Andy Card—actually, I was in a classroom talking about a reading program that works. I was sitting outside the classroom waiting to go in, and I saw an airplane hit the tower—the TV was obviously on. And I used to fly, myself, and I said, well, there's one terrible pilot. I said, it must have been a horrible accident. But I was whisked off there, I didn't have much time to think about it. And I was sitting in the classroom, and Andy Card, my chief of staff, who is sitting over here, walked in and said, 'A second plane has hit the tower. America is under attack.'" What is bizarre about this recollection?

A. The Florida coincidence.

B. His confusion about where in the school he was.

C. His thinking, "Well, there's one terrible pilot."

D. All of the above, plus the fact that it couldn't possibly have happened as he recalls it.

ANSWER: D. Actually, pretty much every word of it is inspired lunacy. First, there's the big fuss he makes over the small Florida coincidence. Then, he's in the classroom, he's outside the classroom—where is he? Who knows? And he has to say that he saw it on TV—as opposed to where? On the blackboard? Then he recalls his own flying days, has that hilarious "terrible pilot" moment—*he* would never have been so stupid!—and says he really "didn't have much time to think about it" because he was "whisked off" somewhere, which is wild because, really, how could you see that and not think about it? But the best part is that he's claiming to have seen the first plane hit the tower live on TV, which no one else in the world did, but who knows, maybe if you're the president you get things like the World Trade Center channel.

4. In the days following September 11, what prompted White House press secretary Ari Fleischer to say, "The reminder is to all Americans that they need to watch what they say, watch what they do, and that this is not a time for remarks like that. It never is"?

A. *Politically Incorrect* host Bill Maher's observation that, crazy as they doubtless were, Mohammad Atta and his pals were also kind of brave, whereas "We have been the cowards, lobbing cruise missiles from two thousand miles away. That's cowardly."

B. *New York Observer* columnist Nicholas von Hoffman's reference to George W. Bush as "this little man who is too small for his suits. Him with his stumblings, his swarm of meaningless phrases, his *make no mistake about it*s. Make no mistake about it, this shrimp, this sea urchin is not up to the job."

C. Tina Fey's *Saturday Night Live* joke that Geraldo Rivera's becoming a war correspondent in Afghanistan "raises an interesting ethical question: Do we have to act sad if Geraldo dies?"

D. Jerry Falwell's claim that various liberal groups had angered God and thus allowed "the enemies of America to give us probably what we deserve."

ANSWER: A.

5. Before virtually disappearing for a long while after September 11, how much time had Dick Cheney been spending with George W. Bush during a typical day in the White House?

A. They almost never saw each other.

B. They had lunch three times a week.

C. He stopped by the Oval Office a few times a day to, as he put it, "share a chuckle or two."

D. He spent half the day or more with Bush, attending his intelligence and policy briefings and sitting close by him during his meetings with congressmen, senators, and foreign leaders.

ANSWER: D.

6. What states did Air Force One stop in on its less-than-direct route back to Washington from Florida on September 11?

A. Louisiana and Nebraska

B. Mississippi and Arkansas

C. Texas and Tennessee

D. Oregon and Maine

ANSWER: A. The official line was that Air Force One had been targeted by terrorists, but it turned out there was not one iota of evidence to back up this claim.

7. What word best describes George W. Bush's demeanor as he attempted to reassure the nation in the hours following the attacks?

A. Steady

B. Confident

C. Inspiring

D. Unreassuring

ANSWER: D. Also, shaky, skittish, nervous, and anything else a thesaurus might have to offer under "fear," or "anxiety." As one observer noted about the comparative behavior of Bush and New York's Rudy Giuliani, "Giuliani seemed presidential and Bush aspired to seeming mayoral."

8. Ari Fleischer said that the end result of an executive order signed by George W. Bush allowing a sitting president to keep the papers of a previous president secret—even if that other president wants to make them public—would be that "more information will be forthcoming." TRUE OR FALSE?

ANSWER: True. Said presidential historian Hugh Davis Graham, "Those claims are absurd."

9. Complete George W. Bush's bold declaration of determination as he embarked on war in Afghanistan: "We'll be tough and resolute as we unite, to make sure freedom stands, to rout out evil, to say to our children and grandchildren, we were bold enough to act, without tiring, so that you can live in a great land and in a peaceful world. And there's no doubt in my mind, not one doubt in my mind, that _____"

A. our triumph will be one of historical portions.

B. the American people is up to the task.

C. this will be a hard and long-fought struggle, but we will prevail.

D. we will fail.

10. How did George W. Bush describe the perpetrators of September 11?

A. "You've heard of the Fruits of Islam? These are the Nuts of Islam."

B. "Those folks who committed this act."

C. "The Axis of Axes-to-Grind."

D. "The evilest of all evil-doers doing evil ever."

11. Asked by a reporter if he wanted Osama bin Laden dead, George W. Bush responded, "There's an old poster out west, as I recall, that said, 'Wanted Dead or Alive.' " What was Laura Bush's reaction to this?

A. "Preferably the former."

B. "Git 'im, Bushie!"

C. "We'll never find him."

D. "Tone it down, darling."

Headlines

12. Which of these headlines *did not* appear in a daily U.S. newspaper during George W. Bush's third hundred days?

A. "Bastards!"

B. "Horror!"

C. "Hijackers Surprised to Find Selves in Hell"

D. " 'Oh, My God!' "

ANSWER: C. It appeared in the humor weekly *The Onion*, along with such other gems as "God Angrily Clarifies 'Don't Kill' Rule," "U.S. Vows to Defeat Whoever It Is We're at War With," and "A Shattered Nation Longs to Care About Stupid Bullshit Again."

Quiz #16

The Fourth Hundred Days

Enronmania

1. What did Treasury Secretary Paul O'Neill have to say about the Enron collapse?

   A. "You've seen one 'biggest corporate bankruptcy in history,' you've seen them all."
   B. "Companies come and go. It's part of the genius of capitalism."
   C. "In a year or two, we'll be laughing at this."
   D. "[It's] a tribute to American capitalism."

ANSWER: **B.** And George W. Bush's top economic adviser Larry Lindsey said **D.** Enron's chairman, Kenneth Lay, actually said **C.** to a group of employees who were skeptical that they'd ever find losing their life savings all that funny.

2. Which Enron-related lie did George W. Bush tell?

A. He claimed that Enron chairman Kenneth Lay "was a supporter of Ann Richards" in the 1994 Texas gubernatorial race, though Lay actually gave three times as much money to Bush and even declared for him.
B. He implied that Lay was a Richards administration holdover that he first "got to know" after being elected governor, though they'd actually worked together on the 1992 Republican convention, and he knew him well enough to have given him the nickname "Kenny Boy."
C. He expressed outrage that his own mother-in-law bought $8,000 worth of Enron stock "last summer," though she'd actually purchased it in 1999.
D. All of the above.

ANSWER: D.

3. Whose fury at the press for actually doing its job and energetically covering the Enron scandal—only the largest bankruptcy in history—prompted her to blurt on *Imus in the Morning*, "They act like there's some billing records or some cattle scam or some fired travel aides or some blue dress"?

A. White House counselor Karen Hughes
B. White House aide Mary Matalin
C. Second Lady Lynne Cheney
D. Right wing pundit Ann Coulter

ANSWER: B.

How Many, How Much?

Match the number with what it represents.

4. Clemencies—out of almost nine hundred requested—granted by George W. Bush in 2001.

5. Dollars an Enron share was worth when trading in the stock was suspended.

6. Dollars spent on heavy blue drapes to hide the bare-breasted statue—*Spirit of Justice,* there since 1936—that John Ashcroft hated to have his head photographed under when he spoke at the (apparently unmovable) Justice Department podium.

7. Dogs that saw George W. Bush faint, tumble off his couch, smack his head on a coffee table, and bruise his face after incorrectly eating a pretzel.

    A. 0
    B. .67
    C. 2
    D. 8,650

ANSWERS: 4-A, 5-B, 6-D, 7-C. And the pretzel incident—about which the *London Daily Telegraph* wrote, "This is exactly the sort of accident that befalls Homer Simpson, night after night"—occurred almost ten years to the day after Bush's father threw up on the Japanese prime minister at a state dinner in Tokyo.

Who?

8. Who is David Frum?

    A. The White House budget director who referred to New York's refusal to settle for 55 percent of

George W. Bush's promised $20 million in reconstruction aid as "a little money-grubbing game."

B. The magazine columnist who called George W. Bush "a playground bully cleaned up for church."

C. The Republican governor who joked that George W. Bush is "the only guy in history who had to take lessons to get that smirk off his face."

D. The White House speechwriter who came up with the phrase "axis of evil."

ANSWER: D. Well, two-thirds of it, anyway—he had "axis of hatred" and it got changed. And then his proud wife sent an e-mail to friends and family claiming credit for him for this deathless blip of prose, and the e-mail wound up in *State*, and he wound up losing his job, after which he rushed out the Bush White House's first memoir. Mitch Daniels is the snarky budget director. *New York* magazine's Michael Wolff called Bush a bully. South Dakota's William Janklow is the governor who went on to Congress in 2003 and quickly resigned after being convicted of involuntary manslaughter for speeding through a stop sign and killing a motorcyclist.

9. "To those who scare peace-loving people with phantoms of lost liberty, my message is this: Your tactics only aid terrorists." Who issued this warning to anyone who was even contemplating protesting the assault on civil liberties?

A. White House press secretary Ari Fleischer
B. Defense Secretary Donald Rumsfeld
C. Attorney General John Ashcroft
D. Supreme Court Justice Antonin Scalia

ANSWER: C

What?

10. What prompted Hillary Clinton to say of George W. Bush, "That's clever"?

A. His nicknaming Tennessee senator Bill Frist "Fristy."
B. His nicknaming Donald Rumsfeld "Rummy."
C. His nicknaming Florida congressman Mark Foley "Foleyman."
D. His nicknaming Arkansas senator Tim Hutchinson "Hutch."

ANSWER: C.

The Terror, The Terror

11. What did George W. Bush say when asked by a reporter whether the war on terrorism had changed him?

A. "I believe it has. I believe it's made me a bit more bloodthirsty."
B. "It's pretty much allowed me to do whatever I want in the name of homeland security."
C. "Talk to my wife. I don't know. I don't spend a lot of time looking in the mirror. Except when I comb my hair."
D. "I'll tell you this. I sure got to say 'evildoers' a lot more than I would have otherwise."

ANSWER: C.

12. Which of George W. Bush's tough guy pronouncements actually made no sense as a tough guy pronouncement?

A. His declaration that Osama Bin Laden was "Wanted Dead or Alive."

B. His response to onlookers at the fallen World Trade Center who said they couldn't hear him: "I can hear you. The rest of the world hears you. And the people who knocked these buildings down will hear all of us soon."

C. His promise to "smoke out" those responsible and "git 'em."

D. His pledge that "Not over my dead body will they raise your taxes!"

ANSWER: D. Really, look at it. It makes *no sense* as any kind of threat.

117

Quiz #17

Bushspeak

1. Complete George W. Bush's statement: "You teach a child to read and _____ will be able to pass a literacy test."

   A. they
   B. he or her
   C. her and him
   D. it

ANSWER: B. Him really said it.

2. George W. Bush made three of these statements. Which one was spoken long ago by his father?

   A. "The way I like to put it is this: There's no bigger issue for the president to remind the moms and dads of America, if you happen to have a child, be fortunate to have a child."

B. "It's appropriate we talk about policy that will affect people's lives in a positive way in which a beautiful, beautiful part of our national—our national—really, our national park system, I guess, is you'd want to call it."

C. "We're enjoying sluggish times, and not enjoying them very much."

D. "It's a country I am so proud to be the president of the United States."

ANSWER: C.

3. Three of these statements were uttered by George W. Bush. Which one is a 1990 Quaylism?

A. "Home is important. It's important to have a home."

B. "For NASA, space is still a high priority."

C. "I respect the Hispanic culture a lot."

D. "I am mindful not only of preserving executive powers for myself, but for predecessors as well."

ANSWER: B.

4. Complete George W. Bush's response when asked what Independence Day meant to him: "Well, it's an unimaginable honor to be the president during the Fourth of July of this country. It means what these words say, for starters. The great inalienable rights of our country. We're blessed with such values in America. And I—it's—I'm a proud man to be the nation based upon such wonderful values. I can't tell you what it's like to be in Europe, for example, to be talking about the greatness of America. But the true greatness of America _____ "

A. can be found in the humor of Triumph the Insult Comic Dog.

B. is that we still allow, heh-heh, sorry, don't know why I'm laughin', heh-heh, executions.

C. is the fact that anyone can grow up to be president—even the guy who lost the election.

D. are the people.

ANSWER: D.

5. Three of these statements were spoken by George W. Bush. Which one is a 1989 Quaylism?

A. "It's negative to think about blowing each other up. That's not a positive thought. That's a Cold War thought. That's a thought when people were enemies with each other."

B. "Africa is a nation that suffers from incredible disease."

C. "The amazing thing about this job is the job seems to follow you around."

D. "This administration stands for the future. It also stands for what's good about this country."

ANSWER D.

6. George W. Bush uttered three of these sentences. Which one popped out of Dan Quayle's mouth in 1988?

A. "An equal society begins with an equally excellent schools."

B. "We're going to have the best-educated American people in the world."

C. "I want to thank all the adults who are telling the children they love them."

D. "Fathers have a unique and irreplaceable role in the lives of children."

ANSWER: B.

7. What kind of rights did George W. Bush say are given to the American people in the Declaration of Independence?

A. "Securitized"
B. "Unalienable"
C. "Inalienable"
D. "Uninalienable"

ANSWER: D.

8. What was George W. Bush's explanation for why he named the Justice Department building after Robert F. Kennedy?

A. "Because the Kennedys always depreciate honors like that."
B. "Because he's deservant."
C. "Because there was no public upswell for Edwin Meese."
D. "Because he was a man who worked there who was assassinated."

ANSWER: B.

9. Three of these thoughts were given voice by George W. Bush. Which was spoken by Defense Secretary Donald Rumsfeld?

A. "There's nothing more deep than recognizing Israel's right to exist. That's the most deep thought of all. . . . I can't think of anything more deep than that right."

B. "I'm not into this detail stuff. I'm more concepty."

C. "And so, in my State of the . . . my State of the Union—or state—my speech to the nation, whatever you want to call it, speech to the nation . . . I asked Americans to give four thousand years—four thousand hours over the next . . . the rest of your life . . . of service to America."

D. "This is a nation that loves our freedom, loves our country."

ANSWER: B.

10. Standing in front of a panorama of giant redwoods, George W. Bush said those trees were there when the Magna Carta was signed. TRUE OR FALSE?

ANSWER: False. He said they were there when the "Magna Carter" was signed.

Quiz #18

The Critics Speak

1. Complete *Wall Street Journal* columnist Peggy Noonan's observation about George W. Bush: "His eyes are close together and dark, two little _____ on a beige muffin, and they both sparkle and are unexpressive."

A. raisins
B. watermelon seeds
C. roaches
D. black holes

ANSWER: A.

2. Complete retired logging equipment salesman Walter Taylor's observation about George W. Bush: "He's not the kind of guy I'd like to sit on the bank and fish with. I'd like to _____"

A. maybe have dinner with him, talk a little baseball.

B. be anywhere in the universe but there.

C. get invited to the White House, though.

D. throw him in the water.

ANSWER: D. Taylor told *The New York Times*, "He doesn't look like a leader, either. He looks like a spoiled kid who wouldn't know what to do if we get into a real international jam."

3. "George W. Bush is like a bad comic working the crowd, a moron, if you'll pardon the expression." Who said it?

A. Martin Sheen

B. Alec Baldwin

C. Tim Robbins

D. Janeane Garofalo

ANSWER: A.

4. Complete *USA Today* TV critic Robert Bianco's observation about George W. Bush: "He has to stop drawing his eyebrows together too closely to convey seriousness; it makes him look _____"

A. like he's got a migraine.

B. like something out of Dr. Seuss.

C. like an owl about to pounce.

D. like he's daring us to take him seriously.

ANSWER: C.

5. Complete *New York Times* columnist Maureen Dowd's observation about George W. Bush: "The harder it gets, the more squarely he is confronted with his own limitations. And the more squarely W. is confronted with his own limitations, the more rattled and unrelaxed he gets. And the more rattled and unrelaxed he gets, _____ "

A. the more you notice just how humongous those limitations are.
B. the more you wonder just what it is that makes this spoiled brat think he's so entitled to his nasty little 'tude.
C. the more rattled and unrelaxed he gets.
D. the more you think, *"I'd* be out drinking, too, if *this* was *my* dad."

ANSWER: C.

6. Complete NAACP chairman Julian Bond's observation about George W. Bush: "He has selected nominees from the Taliban wing of American politics, appeased the wretched appetites of the extreme right wing, and chosen cabinet officials whose devotion to the Confederacy is nearly _____ in its uncritical affection."

A. feline
B. bovine
C. canine
D. asinine

ANSWER: C.

Who said what about George W. Bush?

7. "He's a terrible ignoramus."
8. "He is the anti-Christ."
9. "I have been disappointed in almost everything he has done."

A. Former president Jimmy Carter

B. Actor Robert Redford

C. Environmental activist Bianca Jagger

ANSWERS: 7-B, 8-C, 9-A.

10. Complete *L.A. Weekly* columnist Harold Meyerson's observation about George W. Bush: "The restoration is upon us. _____ now rules, to a general, still largely unspoken sense of incredulity. The thought that will not go away, even among Republicans for whom W.'s legitimacy is not at issue, is: What is he doing there?"

A. The least qualified man in our lifetimes

B. The world's oldest sullen teenager

C. The dynasty's dullard son

D. Incurious George

ANSWER: C. Meyerson also wrote, "You have to go back to Coolidge to find a president with a résumé so short, a presence so uninspiring, an intelligence so difficult to locate. . . . Bush himself seems to be wondering, *What am I doing here?* For Clinton, the presidency was the supreme object of his desire; for Bush, it seems more like a chore he's been unable to duck. Thirty years after he got out of going to Vietnam, the draft has finally caught up with him."

126

Quiz #19

The Fifth Hundred Days

Recriminations

1. Though George W. Bush had been warned in early August about the possibility of airplane-related terrorism in the United States, White House officials claim that the reason it took eight months for this fact to come to light is that no one really remembered having been warned until recently. TRUE OR FALSE?

ANSWER: True.

2. Who is Kenneth Williams?

A. The NBC reporter whose putting a question to Jacques Chirac in his native French prompted George W. Bush to sneer, "The guy memorizes four words and he plays like he's intercontinental."

B. The Phoenix FBI agent who wrote the famously ignored memo warning that terrorists might be training at American flight schools.

C. The INS inspector in charge of the investigation looking into how visa approval notices were belatedly sent to two September 11 hijackers.

D. The EPA civil enforcement chief who resigned because he felt that he was "fighting a White House that seems determined to weaken the rules we are trying to enforce."

ANSWER: **B.** NBC's David Gregory was the big linguistic show-off. Glenn A. Fine was the INS inspector. Eric Schaeffer was the disgruntled EPA official.

3. Five weeks after White House spokesman Ari Fleischer implied that Bill Clinton was to blame for the current violence in the Middle East, and was forced to retract the implication, George W. Bush implied that Bill Clinton was to blame for the current violence in the Middle East, and was forced to retract the implication. TRUE OR FALSE?

ANSWER: True.

4. What was Defense Secretary Donald Rumsfeld's response when asked if he wanted Osama bin Laden dead?

A. "I want to use his head for a bowling ball."
B. "Would I be sorry if he turned up dead? No."
C. "Oh, my goodness gracious, yes."
D. "Heavens to Betsy, no."

ANSWER: C.

The Music Men

5. Which Bush administration wife did Eminem say "Fuck you" to on "White America"?

   A. Laura Bush
   B. Lynne Cheney
   C. Janet Ashcroft
   D. Darby Rove

ANSWER: B. "Ms. Cheney" to him.

6. What did Ozzy Osbourne shout to George W. Bush at the White House Correspondents' Association dinner?

   A. "Guess who watches me—fuckin' Quayle!"
   B. "Don't wave at Stevie Wonder, he's fuckin' blind!"
   C. "Put Bono on the fuckin' ticket, man!"
   D. "You should wear your hair like mine!"

ANSWER: D.

In Print

7. How does the first chapter of Frank Bruni's book *Ambling into History: The Unlikely Odyssey of George W. Bush* begin?

   A. Young George W. Bush gets a zero on the first paper he hands in at Phillips Academy in Andover. The paper—a sad story about the death of his younger sister when he was seven—is called "disgraceful" by his professor because Bush, having

found an impressive substitute for "tears" in the thesaurus, wrote, "Lacerates ran down my cheeks."
B. George W. Bush's father tells him, "I just want you to know you have disappointed me" after young Bush has left his job on a Louisiana oil rig a week early, assuming that no one would notice.
C. Texas governor George W. Bush is making goofy faces at the press while attending a service for seven people slaughtered in a church by a lunatic gunman.
D. Presidential candidate George W. Bush gets really furious on his campaign plane when he finds that someone has eaten his peanut butter and jelly sandwich.

ANSWER: C. All the other things happened, too, of course.

8. According to the German magazine *Der Spiegel,* what prompted Brazilian president Fernando Henrique Cardoso to observe that George W. Bush is "still learning"?

A. His unenforceable demand that Israel withdraw from the West Bank.
B. His administration's clumsy handling of the failed Venezuelan coup.
C. His policy reversals on steel tariffs and farm subsidies.
D. His asking Cardoso, "Do you have blacks, too?" thus revealing his ignorance of the fact that Brazil has the largest black population of any non-African nation.

ANSWER: D.

Headlines

9. Which headline *did not* appear in a U.S. daily news-paper during George W. Bush's fifth hundred days?

A. "EPA Would Allow Mine Dumping in Waterways"
B. "Cheney on 9/11: 'We Blew It Big-Time' "
C. "In Shift, Justice Dept. Pushes to Widen Rights to Own Guns"
D. "White House Cut 93% of Funds Sought to Guard Atomic Arms"

ANSWER: B.

Blast from the Past

10. Explaining why the Israeli-Palestinian crisis should not be confused with the U.S. war on terrorism, Dan Quayle said, "How many Palestinians were on those airplanes on September 11? None." TRUE OR FALSE?

ANSWER: False. He said, "How many Palestinians were on those airplanes on September 9?"

Quiz #20

The Sixth Hundred Days

Warnings

1. Which member of his father's administration wrote a *Wall Street Journal* op-ed piece listing all the reasons why "an attack on Iraq at this time would seriously jeopardize, if not destroy, the global counterterrorist campaign we have undertaken"?

A. Former secretary of state James A. Baker III
B. Former national security adviser Brent Scowcroft
C. Former secretary of state Lawrence Eagleburger
D. Former attorney general Richard Thornburgh

ANSWER: B.

2. Which Republican senator said, "You can take the country into a war pretty fast, but you can't get out as quickly, and the public needs to know what the risks are"?

A. Nebraska's Chuck Hagel
B. Maine's Olympia Snowe
C. Alabama's Richard Shelby
D. Indiana's Richard Lugar

ANSWER: A. Hagel, a consistently perceptive Bush critic, later said, "We cannot afford to shrug off negative public opinion overseas as uninformed or irrelevant. . . . The responsibility of leadership is to persuade, not to impugn the motives of those who disagree with you."

Meeting the Press

3. To what was George W. Bush referring when he said at a press conference, "Sometimes things aren't exactly black and white"?

A. Evolution vs. creationism
B. Executing retarded prisoners
C. A questionable stock sale he'd been involved in twelve years earlier
D. Whether he thought Osama bin Laden was a bad man

ANSWER: C. The full statement was, "In the corporate world, sometimes things aren't exactly black and white when it comes to accounting procedures." After he said it, reporters tittered, and he glared at them. He also pointed out that there was no "malfeasance" (accent on the mal) involved.

4. As he was about to start a round of golf, George W. Bush took a moment to comment on a suicide bus bombing that had just killed nine in Israel, saying, "I call upon all nations to do everything they can to stop these terrorist killings." What did he do next?

A. He launched into an eloquent attack on the cruelty of random killing that those who heard it claimed was one of his finest moments.

B. He vowed that he would "not rest until every last terrorist is rounded up from the face of the earth."

C. He said, "You know what? Now I'm not in the mood for golf."

D. Without missing a beat, he added, "Thank you. Now watch this drive," and immediately teed off.

ANSWER: D.

5. George W. Bush gave an interview to the magazine *Runner's World* in which he noted that he'd been "running slower since the war began." TRUE OR FALSE?

ANSWER: False. He actually said, "It's interesting that my times have become faster right after the war began. They were pretty fast all along, but since the war began I have been running with a little more intensity." As *New York Times* columnist Maureen Dowd wrote, "So the bad news is: We haven't caught Osama. The good news is: W.'s times have improved."

6. What question occurred to *New York Times* columnist Maureen Dowd as she watched George W. Bush on TV going on about exercise and nutrition?

A. "Why is the most fitness-crazed president in the nation's history sometimes so short on stamina?"

B. "Why does someone who bench presses 185 pounds still have an aura that's more scrawny than brawny?"

134

C. "Why does the leader of the free world, a man with limitless possibilities for stimulation, seem to get really jazzed only when he can run his 6:45 miles?"

D. All of the above.

ANSWER: D.

7. Complete George W. Bush's observation to Associated Press reporter Scott Lindlaw during a tour of his Crawford, Texas, ranch: "Most Americans don't _____ "

A. care about anything that happens more than a mile or two from where they live.

B. sit in Martha's Vineyard, swilling white wine.

C. remember that I didn't really win.

D. want to think about what this country's going to look like after eight years of me.

ANSWER: B.

8. When a reporter asked why he wasn't attending the NAACP meeting in Houston, George W. Bush scornfully pointed out that Colin Powell and Condoleezza Rice are in his inner circle. TRUE OR FALSE?

ANSWER: True. Some of his best friends . . .

Blanks

9. Complete the complaint about the French that George W. Bush was reported to have shared with British prime minister Tony Blair, only to have Blair's

135

people deny it when the story broke: "The problem with the French is that _____"

A. they think their shit don't stink.

B. they don't have a word for entrepreneur.

C. they don't smoke enough cigarettes.

D. they're so damn portentious.

ANSWER: B.

10. Complete George W. Bush's defiant statement about the terrorists: "They will not _____"

A. tie America hostage.

B. hold America blackmail.

C. squeeze America hostile.

D. blow America down.

ANSWER: B.

Quiz #21

The Seventh Hundred Days

Give War a Chance

1. Who explained that the Bush administration waited until September to push publicly for war with Iraq because "from a marketing point of view, you don't introduce new products in August"?

    A. Attorney General John Ashcroft
    B. Chief of staff Andrew Card
    C. Press secretary Ari Fleischer
    D. National security adviser Condoleezza Rice

ANSWER: B.

2. How did George W. Bush refer to Saddam Hussein?

    A. "Saddam Hitler."
    B. "A man who, if he didn't cause 9/11, well, he might as well have."

137

C. "You know how when I like someone I say, 'He's a good man'? This is a bad man. Him I don't like."

D. "A guy that tried to kill my dad."

ANSWER: D. And isn't that really the nub of it?

3. Who made the perceptive observation that Osama bin Laden was "either alive and well or alive and not too well or not alive"?

A. Dick Cheney
B. Donald Rumsfeld
C. Ari Fleischer
D. John Ashcroft

ANSWER: B.

4. Who suggested that it wouldn't be a bad thing if some enterprising Iraqi decided to kill Saddam Hussein?

A. Donald Rumsfeld
B. Condoleezza Rice
C. Ari Fleischer
D. Dick Cheney

ANSWER: C. "Regime change is welcome in whatever form it takes," he said, and "the cost of one bullet, if the Iraqi people take it on themselves, is substantially less" than going to war.

Ari Sucks

5. Who said Ari Fleischer was not merely an uncommonly unforthcoming White House press secretary but had "the uncanny ability to suck information out of a room"?

A. CBS's John Roberts
B. NBC's Campbell Brown

C. ABC's Terry Moran
D. CNN's John King

ANSWER: A.

Woodward

6. Complete George W. Bush's statement to reporter Bob Woodward for his book *Bush at War:* "I loathe _____"

A. [France's president] Jacques Chirac.
B. [Germany's chancellor] Gerhard Schroder.
C. everyone who ever said anything bad about me, and I mean *everyone* who *ever* said *anything,* every single person, everyone from Al Gore to some guy in Texas who criticized my health care policies to some kid in third grade who made fun of my ears, and you know what? Whenever I hear that anything bad happened to any of them—and I do, I hear, because I have a list and, maybe you've noticed, I'm the president, so people keep track for me—when I hear that one of them lost a job, or one of their kids didn't get into the college he wanted to, or maybe somebody's house caught fire and they lost all their belongings, I *laugh my ass off.*"
D. [North Korea's leader] Kim Jong Il.

ANSWER: D.

7. What did George W. Bush tell Bob Woodward about the conversational give-and-take of high-level meetings?

A. "You'd be surprised how many different things you have to think about."

B. "Lots of times someone will say something smart or decisive-sounding, and then I'll wink and say, 'The president said that,' and lo and behold, in the newspaper stories the quote is attributed to me."
C. "I'm the commander—see, I don't need to explain—I do not need to explain why I say things. That's the interesting thing about being the president. Maybe somebody needs to explain to me why they say something, but I don't feel like I owe anybody an explanation."
D. "You know what's a kick? Reaming someone out when a cell phone rings. Sometimes I find myself sitting there bored out of my mind in one of these meetings, and I'm thinking, 'If only someone's phone goes off I can have some fun.' "

ANSWER: C.

Oops

8. What happened the same day that George W. Bush gave a speech announcing that the AmeriCorps national service program was "expanding mightily"?

A. The first ever AmeriCorps volunteer passed away.
B. Laura Bush suggested that Jenna and Barbara "might want to consider" giving a year of their lives to it.
C. The program announced that lack of funds was causing it to freeze recruitment of volunteers.

D. Dick Cheney gave a speech pooh-poohing volunteerism as "a nice guilt assuager, but it's not going to change the world."

ANSWER: C.

9. What reason did George W. Bush give for Laura being unable to attend an event during their summer stay at the ranch in Crawford, Texas?

A. "She melted."
B. "She needs to sweep the porch."
C. "She's got the curse."
D. "Somebody has to stay home in case we need to bail out the girls."

ANSWER: B.

Preemptive Strike

10. Which cartoonist ran a strip in which George W. Bush announces, "Because the moon *may* someday break out of orbit and crash into the Earth, I have decided to use our nookyalur arsenal to destroy it now"?

A. David Rees in *Get Your War On*
B. Garry Trudeau in *Doonesbury*
C. Tom Tomorrow in *This Modern World*
D. Matt Groening in *Life in Hell*

ANSWER: C.

Quiz #22

Domestic Affairs

The Economy

1. Which children's story did George W. Bush evoke in his defense of his tax cut?

    A. "Goldilocks and the Three Bears"
    B. "Little Red Riding Hood"
    C. "The Three Little Pigs"
    D. *Alice in Wonderland*

ANSWER: A. He said, "Some say it's too large, some say it's too small. I say it's just right."

2. How does George W. Bush often refer to the estate tax?

    A. "The real estate tax"
    B. "The estate sales tax"

C. "The death tax"

D. "The double dip"

ANSWER: C. Or, if he's totally flummoxed, "the death penalty."

3. When critics of his tax cuts pointed out that the wealthiest 1 percent of taxpayers will divvy up 28 percent of the windfall, while the poorest 60 percent will split 8 percent of the benefits, George W. Bush accused them of engaging in "class warfare." TRUE OR FALSE?

ANSWER: True. Not to mention, when was the last time we saw a president push for a tax cut as he embarked on a war? Like, maybe *never?*

4. Barring an unimaginable economic miracle that would trigger the creation of almost 3 million new jobs in less than a year, George W. Bush will end this term as the first president since Jimmy Carter to oversee a net loss in unemployment. TRUE OR FALSE?

ANSWER: False. He'll be the first president since Herbert Hoover to have this distinction.

5. Which senators were attacked in TV spots, doubtlessly if unprovably conceived in the White House, as "so-called Republicans" for having the sheer temerity to oppose George W. Bush's third round of tax cuts?

A. Olympia Snowe (R-Maine) and George Voinovich (R-Ohio)

B. Pete Domenici (R-N.M.) and John McCain (R-Ariz.)

C. Charles Grassley (R-Iowa) and Chuck Hagel (R-Neb.)

143

D. Lincoln Chafee (R-R.I.) and Richard Lugar (R-Ind.)

6. According to Dick Cheney, why was the wildly ballooning deficit not a cause for concern?

A. Because the government could "turn it around overnight if we play our cards right" in John Poindexter's terrorism futures market.

B. Because "if we need to, we can always borrow a few trillion from Halliburton."

C. Because "I am a deficit hawk," and, even more reassuring, "so is the president."

D. Because "the world could blow up tomorrow, and then all debts would be forgiven and we'd look pretty damn smart."

The Environment

7. Referring to the controversy about arsenic levels in drinking water at a dinner for radio and TV correspondents, George W. Bush joked, "To base our decision on sound science, the scientists told us we needed to test the water glasses of about three thousand people. Thank you for participating." TRUE OR FALSE?

8. Which headline *did not* appear in a daily U.S. newspaper during George W. Bush's first hundred days?

A. "Bush to Delay Plan for Clean Waterways"
B. "Bush Picks Industry Insiders to Fill Environmental Posts"
C. "Bush Signs Repeal of Ergonomics Rules; Administration Promises Business-Friendly Workplace Safety Regulations"
D. "Nader: 'I Goofed' "

ANSWER: D. *Au contraire*, when asked about the egregious economic, environmental, and international policies Bush was only getting to implement thanks to Nader's campaign, he replied, "I'm just amazed that people think I should be concerned about this stuff. When his offer to testify against John Ashcroft at his confirmation hearings was ignored by Senate Democrats, Nader's obtuse response was, "There's some pretty foolish ostracism going on." Two things seem certain: he will never offer one syllable of contrition, and he will never be forgiven.

9. How did White House chief of staff Andrew Card describe George W. Bush's meeting with California governor Gray Davis to discuss his state's energy crisis?

A. "They talked about governor stuff. Remember, the president was a governor, too."
B. "Not the smoothest encounter of the year, but everyone survived."
C. "The president mentioned how badly he'd done in California and asked the governor, 'How much help would *you* give you if you were me?' "
D. "A very friendly meeting—it was candid. It was a very, very friendly and constructive

conversation. . . . It started off very friendly. I mean, it was a very, very friendly conversation."

ANSWER: D. And what happened after all that sweetness and light? Davis announced that he was suing the federal government.

10. Asked whether George W. Bush felt that Americans needed to cut back on their excessive energy consumption, press secretary Ari Fleischer said, "The president feels that this is probably the number one thing Americans can do to help the war on terrorism." TRUE OR FALSE?

ANSWER: False. Fleischer actually responded, "That's a big no. The President believes that it's an American way of life, and that it should be the goal of policy makers to protect the American way of life. The American way of life is a blessed one."

Quiz #23

Ashcroft

Background Check

1. Who is Paul Offner?

A. The man who testified that John Ashcroft once started off a job interview with him by asking, "Do you have the same sexual preferences as most men?"

B. The black Missouri Supreme Court judge whose appointment to the federal bench Ashcroft blocked in the Senate by falsely claiming he'd shown "a tremendous bent toward criminal activity" and was "pro-criminal" (though a Missouri police organization had endorsed him for a judgeship) and had a "poor record on the death penalty" (though out of fifty-two appeals heard, he'd voted to uphold the death penalty in forty-one cases, and voted with the majority in ten cases to reverse it because of legal error).

C. The gay man whose appointment by President Clinton as ambassador to Luxembourg Senator Ashcroft tried to block.

D. The editor of *Southern Partisan,* a virulently racist publication that defends slavery and apartheid, and which Ashcroft has praised for helping to "set the record straight."

ANSWER: A. Ronnie White was the judge, James Hormel was the ambassador whom Clinton appointed while Congress was in recess, and Christopher M. Sullivan edits *Southern Partisan.* In the course of defending the magazine, Ashcroft said, "We've got to stand up and speak in this respect, or else we'll be taught that these people were giving their lives, subscribing their sacred fortunes and their honor to some perverted agenda." Translation: Slavery was not a perverted agenda.

2. While sitting in judgment of President Clinton in his 1999 impeachment trial, then-senator John Ashcroft rented out his political action committee's fund-raising list to snitch Linda Tripp. **TRUE OR FALSE?**

ANSWER: True.

3. From which college did John Ashcroft receive an honorary degree in 1999?

A. Hampshire College
B. Columbia University
C. Stanford University
D. Bob Jones University

ANSWER: D.

148

Thanks!

4. Which eight Senate Democrats voted to confirm John Ashcroft as Attorney General?

   A. Delaware's Joseph Biden, Iowa's Tom Harkin, Maryland's Paul Sarbanes and Barbara Mikulski, Massachusetts's Edward Kennedy, Minnesota's Paul Wellstone, New York's Charles Schumer, and Vermont's Patrick Leahy
   B. Connecticut's Chris Dodd, Georgia's Zell Miller, Louisiana's John Breaux, Nebraska's Ben Nelson, North Dakota's Kent Conrad and Byron Dorgan, West Virginia's Robert Byrd, and Wisconsin's Russ Feingold
   C. California's Barbara Boxer and Dianne Feinstein, Florida's Bob Graham, Georgia's Max Cleland, Illinois's Richard Durbin, Montana's Max Baucus, New Mexico's Jeff Bingaman, and South Carolina's Ernest Hollings
   D. Michigan's Carl Levin, Missouri's Jean Carnahan, Nevada's Harry Reid, North Carolina's John Edwards, Oregon's Ron Wyden, South Dakota's Tim Johnson, Washington's Patty Murray and Maria Cantwell

ANSWER: B.

Patriot Act

5. Of the 762 illegal immigrants who were locked up by John Ashcroft's Justice Department in the wake of the September 11 attacks—many of whom were held incommunicado for months, denied access to lawyers or other visitors, kept in solitary confinement, and physically assaulted—how many were ultimately linked to terrorist activities?

A. 573
B. 212
C. 48
D. Not a single one. Zero. Zilch. Nada.

ANSWER: D.

6. What was John Ashcroft's statement to all those people wrongly held?

A. "Better safe than sorry."
B. "We make no apologies."
C. "Tough times make for tough laws."
D. "Hey, anyone can make 762 mistakes."

ANSWER: B.

7. What was Attorney General John Ashcroft unwilling to do in the war against terrorism?

A. Allow federal investigators to listen in on attorney-client conversations.
B. Lengthen the time illegal immigrants can be held without being charged.
C. Allow the FBI to have access to Justice Department records from gun background checks.
D. Allow the government to spy on Web surfing, even of people who are not the target of an investigation.

ANSWER: C. But everything else—no problem.

Terrorism Can Wait

8. What did a U.S. district judge reprimand John Ashcroft for?

A. His repeated efforts to criminalize Oregon doctors who are obeying a state law allowing physician-assisted suicide.
B. His refusal to allow gay Justice Department employees to hold a Gay Pride event at work.
C. His allowing Microsoft to avoid a breakup.
D. His rabid pursuit of death penalty prosecutions.

ANSWER: A.

9. The September 11 attacks and the urgent demands on law enforcement officials that resulted from them were not enough to get John Ashcroft to call off a thirteen-month Justice Department investigation of a bordello in New Orleans, a city where prostitution is a misdemeanor. After hundreds of pages of surveillance transcripts and reports by ten FBI agents, the investigation resulted in the arrest of nearly two hundred prostitutes. TRUE OR FALSE?

ANSWER: False. All that effort was expended to catch a dozen—yes, a mere twelve—whores.

It's Funny 'Cause It's True

10. Aides to Attorney General John Ashcroft offered as proof of his sense of humor his propensity to lighten the mood at tense meetings with his imitation of which character from *The Simpsons*?

A. Homer
B. Mr. Burns
C. Ned Flanders
D. Apu

ANSWER: B.

Quiz #24

Bush Men

The Adult

1. Who did *New York Times* columnist Bill Keller say was regarded by the international community as "the lone grown-up in an administration with a teenager's twitchy metabolism and self-centered view of the world"?

    A. Secretary of Defense Donald Rumsfeld
    B. Secretary of State Colin Powell
    C. Attorney General John Ashcroft
    D. Dick Cheney

ANSWER: B.

Rove

2. In the spring of 2001, White House aide Karl Rove said, "That would be nice. That would be really nice. That would be really, really nice." What fantasy was he indulging?

   A. China deciding it didn't really need an apology for the spy plane incident after all.
   B. Arnold Schwarzenegger getting elected governor of California.
   C. George W. Bush signing a law making it illegal to be a Democrat.
   D. Strom Thurmond changing his mind and running for a ninth term.

ANSWER: **B.** And then, oh my God, it came true!

3. What stock was Karl Rove still holding more than $100,000 worth of when he met with officials or representatives of that company?

   A. Intel
   B. Pfizer
   C. General Electric
   D. All of the above, plus Johnson & Johnson, Cisco, and Enron.

ANSWER: **D.** before finally selling his portfolio five months after starting work at the White House.

4. One of George W. Bush's two nicknames for Karl Rove is "Boy Genius." What's the other one?

   A. "Karl Marx"
   B. "The Rove Man"

C. "Turd Blossom"
D. "Roveewade"

ANSWER: C.

5. Which college did dropout Karl Rove fail to graduate from?

A. Bob Jones University
B. University of Utah
C. Yale
D. Vassar

ANSWER: B.

Fleischer

6. What was George W. Bush refusing to release that prompted White House spokesman Ari Fleischer to defend the policy by saying, "You know, the very document that protects our liberties more than anything else, the Constitution, was, of course, drafted in total secrecy"?

A. Records of George W. Bush's August 6, 2001, briefing about the Al Qaeda threat to hijack airplanes.
B. Records of his father's dealings with Saddam Hussein.
C. Records of Dick Cheney's secret energy task force meetings.
D. Records of John Ashcroft's secret Patriot Act meetings.

ANSWER: C. As *State* columnist Michael Kinsley wrote of Fleischer, "Most of the reviews dismiss him as an evasive bore. This doesn't give Fleischer nearly enough credit. He is a *great* evasive bore. There's a war on, for heaven's sake. The fate of civilization may be at stake, and your job is to tell the world how the war is going. Under these circumstances, how hard is it to be interesting? On the other hand, to be boring and to stay boring—to maintain your rock-solid commitment to the lack of information while fascinating information cascades from the heavens all around you like emergency food parcels—takes discipline. It takes imagination. Let us not flinch: It takes genius."

7. Ari Fleischer insisted that his earlier statement that he wasn't aware of "anybody in the White House" discussing the Enron situation was technically accurate because, though it turned out that both the treasury secretary and the commerce secretary had had collapse-related conversations with Kenneth Lay after all, neither of them actually worked in the White House itself. TRUE OR FALSE?

ANSWER: True.

Rumsfeld

8. Which of these statements was uttered not by George W. Bush but by Defense Secretary Donald Rumsfeld?

A. "The war on terror involves Saddam Hussein, the history of Saddam Hussein, and his willingness to terrorize himself."
B. "There's no cave deep enough for America, or dark enough to hide."
C. "There are known knowns. These are things we

156

know that we know. There are known unknowns.
That is to say, there are things that we know we
don't know. But there are also unknown unknowns.
There are things we don't know we don't know."

D. "Republicans and Democrats stood with me in
the Rose Garden to announce their support of a
clear statement of purpose [to Hussein]: You
disarm or we will."

ANSWER: C.

9. What was Donald Rumsfeld's response to the looting
of the Iraq Museum?

A. "We didn't allow it to happen. It happened."

B. "Freedom is untidy. Free people are free to make
mistakes and commit crimes and do bad things."

C. "It's the same picture of some person walking
out of some building with a vase, and you see it
twenty times and you think, my goodness, were
there that many vases? Is it possible that there
were that many vases in the whole country?"

D. All of the above.

ANSWER: D. And there's more: "We don't allow bad things to happen. Bad things happen in life, and people do loot." And, "Looting is
an unfortunate thing. . . . No one likes it. No one allows it. It happens, and it's unfortunate."

10. Three of these statements were made by George W.
Bush. Which one was made by Donald Rumsfeld?

A. "Stuff happens."

B. "I think war is a dangerous place."

C. "First, let me make it very clear, poor people

aren't necessarily killers. Just because you happen to be not rich doesn't mean you're willing to kill."

D. "The true strength of America happens when a neighbor loves a neighbor just like they'd like to be loved themselves."

ANSWER: A. Again, about the looting.

11. Three of these statements were uttered by Donald Rumsfeld. Which one was made by George W. Bush?

A. "In Afghanistan, people who are friendly and unfriendly are constantly meeting together. Indeed, sometimes the same people can be friendly and later unfriendly within a relatively short period of time. There are also people who can pretend they're friendly and who, in fact, are not very friendly."

B. "Some of the things will work, some won't, and what we'll do is stop the things that won't and move forward on the things that will."

C. "There is no in-between, as far as I'm concerned. Either you're with us or you're against us."

D. "If something is going to happen, there has to be something for it to happen with that's interested in having it happen."

ANSWER: C.

12. How did one senior army officer respond when he was asked if he likes Donald Rumsfeld?

A. "There's a certain . . . a certain manliness about him that has its appeal, yes."

B. "I know someone who knows someone who likes him."

C. "Do I like him? Sure. Would I like him better if he wasn't always posing questions and then answering them himself? Definitely."

D. " 'Like' is such a strong word."

Quiz #25

The Critics Speak

Who said what about George W. Bush?

1. "He has let his infatuation with his own rectitude metastasize into hubris."

2. "In the months after 9/11, a shocked nation wanted to believe the best of its leader, and Mr. Bush was treated with reverence. But he abused the trust placed in him, pushing a partisan agenda that has left the nation weakened and divided."

3. "Before September 11, I remember asking on TV if Bush knew where Europe was. Then suddenly you had to act as if he was Einstein."

4. "*The [New York] Times* and CNN and others on whom we rely for unvarnished objectivity are telling us . . . 'My God! On September 12 he woke up as Teddy Roosevelt. He became the Rough Rider!' . . .

The media is waving pom-poms, and the entire country is being polite."

   A. *New York Times* columnist Frank Rich
   B. *Weakest Link* host Anne Robinson
   C. *West Wing* creator Aaron Sorkin
   D. *New York Times* columnist Paul Krugman

ANSWERS 1-A, 2-D, 3-B, 4-C.

5. Who wrote, "Living with [Bush] in the Oval Office is like being married to a mate who always says exactly what you know in advance he or she is going to say"?

   A. Martin Amis
   B. Norman Mailer
   C. Gore Vidal
   D. Joan Didion

ANSWER: B.

Who said what about George W. Bush?

6. "When the University of Michigan tries to redress a historic racial injustice by giving some advantage based on race, Mr. Bush gets offended by arbitrarily conferred advantages, as if he himself were not an affirmative-action baby."

7. "He has the unreflective person's immunity from irony, that great killer of intellectual passion. Ask him to reconcile his line on Iraq with his line on North Korea and he just gets irritated."

8. "We are witnessing the tantrum of a woefully untutored and inexperienced president whose willfulness rises in direct proportion to his inability to comprehend a world too complex for his grasp."

9. "There is some kind of anger in the man, a hostility that sometimes seems barely under control—as if he were, in street parlance, being 'dissed.' "

    A. *Slate* columnist Michael Kinsley
    B. *New York Times* columnist Maureen Dowd
    C. Columnist Richard Reeves
    D. *Los Angeles Times* columnist Robert Scheer

ANSWERS: 6-B, 7-A, 8-D, 9-C.

10. Complete comedian Mort Sahl's observation about George W. Bush: "This is the first president _____"

    A. who plays video golf and doesn't read newspapers.
    B. since Ronald Reagan to embrace clearing brush.
    C. who likes to hang out with his father's friends.
    D. who, if you just looked at him and thought, what does this guy do, you'd think of everything else, every other possible occupation in the world, before you'd think 'President of the United States.'

ANSWER: C.

The Eighth Hundred Days

Who?

1. Who is Christopher Lloyd McMillian?

A. The lawyer who was arrested at an Albany mall for refusing to remove a T-shirt bearing the incendiary slogan "Peace on Earth."

B. The Swedish war protester who told British prime minister Tony Blair, "I'm able to produce anthrax in my bathroom. Why don't you bomb Sweden?"

C. The Michigan high school junior who was sent home from school for wearing a T-shirt with a picture of George W. Bush and the words "International Terrorist."

D. A mentally retarded murderer against whom

John Ashcroft was seeking the death penalty even though local prosecutors disagreed.

2. Who called George W. Bush a "populist" and said of him, with a straight face, "Give him a choice between Wall Street and Main Street and he'll choose Main Street every time"?

A. White House adviser Karl Rove
B. Senator Zell Miller (D-Ga.)
C. Commerce Secretary Don Evans
D. Former Montana governor Marc Racicot

3. Who is Jerry Thacker?

A. The Christian conservative who withdrew his nomination to Bush's Advisory Council on HIV and AIDS after it became known that he'd referred to AIDS as the "gay plague" and to homosexuality as a "deathstyle."
B. The poet whose plan to turn a White House poetry symposium into an antiwar protest led First Lady Laura Bush to cancel the event.
C. The commentator who said of Bush's plan to eliminate taxes on stock dividends, "This isn't even trickle-down economics. It's mist-down economics."
D. The White House aide, known for his calm

disposition, about whom Bush adviser Karl Rove said, "I'd use the word 'sweet' if it didn't make me look odd."

Him

4. What was *Washington Post* TV critic Tom Shales's theory about why George W. Bush favors bright blue ties?

A. "Maybe Karl Rove told him it'll win him more votes in the blue states."
B. "Maybe he's afraid a red one would be interpreted as a warning that there could be danger ahead."
C. "Maybe it's his way of giving the finger to the United Nations, as if to say, 'Okay, your flag is blue, but you don't own the color.' "
D. "Maybe he thinks it helps soften the effect of his dark, sharky eyes."

5. Complete George W. Bush's quote: "I've become a guy who really likes _____"

A. power.
B. hating evil.
C. trees.
D. tough guy catchphrases.

6. Which of George W. Bush's tough guy catchphrases turned up in his 2003 State of the Union message?

A. "I'm Sick and Tired of Games and Deception. Time Is Running Out."
B. "The Game Is Over."
C. "However Long It Takes."
D. "[Terrorists we've killed] Are No Longer a Problem."

ANSWER: D. This was the first gloating reference to what might have been extrajudicial killings in the history of State of the Union messages.

7. According to former White House speechwriter David Frum's memoir, *The Right Man,* when George W. Bush found a phrase he considered obvious in a draft of a speech, he sent it back to the writer with the phrase circled and, next to it, the word "Duh." TRUE OR FALSE?

ANSWER: True. Frum wrote that the private Bush "was not the easy, genial man he was in public. Close up, one saw a man keeping a tight grip on himself."

Headlines

8. Which headline *did not* appear in a daily U.S. newspaper during George W. Bush's eighth hundred days?

A. "Bush Orders a 3-Year Delay in Opening Secret Documents"
B. "Terror Advice from Washington: Do Not Seal Doors and Windows"
C. "Bush Asks Congress for More Aid to Poor; Says,

'Why Shouldn't Those Who Actually Need Help Get a Little, Too?' "

D. "Bush Pushes Plan to Curb Appeals in Medicare Cases; Benefit Denials at Issue."

ANSWER: C. Another headline that *did* appear, though, was "Aid to Poor Faces Tighter Scrutiny; Bush Proposes New Tests—Critics See Harm to Needy."

9. Which headline *did not* appear in a daily U.S. newspaper during George W. Bush's eighth hundred days?

A. "Ashcroft Orders U.S. Attorneys to Seek Death in More Cases"

B. "Bush Administration to Seek Exemptions to 2005 Ban of a Pesticide"

C. "Bush Says Size of Protest Gives Him 'Second Thoughts' About Attacking Iraq"

D. "Environmental Penalties Down Under Bush, Data Show"

ANSWER: C. In fact, he scoffed at the protesting millions and said, "Size of protest—it's like deciding, well, I'm going to decide policy based on a focus group." Like he's never done that.

10. Which headline *did not* appear in a daily U.S. newspaper during George W. Bush's eighth hundred days?

A. "Administration Establishes New Wetlands Guidelines; 20 Million Acres Could Lose Protected Status, Groups Say"

B. "Bush Plans to Let Religious Groups Get Building Aid; Worship Sites Involved"

C. "Pentagon Seeking to Deploy Missiles Before Full Testing"

D. "Lieberman Calls Bush 'the Great Squanderer';
Cites Deficit, Jobs, International Goodwill"

ANSWER: D. Lieberman? Come on.

Michaels

11. One problem with Michael Moore's self-righteous rant at the Academy Awards was his failure to acknowledge that, by having supported the candidacy of Ralph Nader and, implicitly, his theory that there was "no difference" between Al Gore and George W. Bush, he bears no small blame for helping to empower the man he now finds so singularly despicable. TRUE OR FALSE?

ANSWER: True.

12. The orange alert of mid-February was returned to yellow after the increased Arab chatter picked up by U.S. intelligence was translated and turned out to be mainly about the Martin Bashir interview with Michael Jackson. TRUE OR FALSE?

ANSWER: False.

Quiz #27

Foreign Affairs

The Big Question

1. What happened during a C-SPAN call-in program that started out as a discussion of George W. Bush's first major foreign policy speech as president?

    A. One of the callers suggested establishing some kind of betting pool to predict the next country for which Bush wouldn't know the name of the leader.
    B. Someone called up to talk about his favorite Bush malaprop (his solution for the economy: "we ought to make the pie higher") and the entire discussion devolved into callers volunteering their personal favorites.
    C. A lesbian activist called in to discuss Bush's meeting with the Log Cabin Republicans, a gay

group that Bush had avoided until he had the nomination sewn up because it might have been a "huge political, you know, nightmare for people."

D. More people called in to talk about whether or not Bush was smirking while he spoke than called in to discuss what he said.

ANSWER: D.

Buddies

2. What was George W. Bush's unexpected response when asked what he and British prime minister Tony Blair had in common?

A. "We once did blow together."

B. "We both use Colgate toothpaste."

C. "We're both illegitimate leaders, except for him."

D. "We both laugh when people is executed."

ANSWER: B, though how he knew remains a mystery.

3. How do British prime minister Tony Blair's critics refer to him in the wake of the Iraq War?

A. "Bush's Toady"

B. "Bush's Lackey"

C. "Bush's Poodle"

D. "Bush's Spittoon"

ANSWER: C.

4. Complete Russian president Vladimir Putin's observation about George W. Bush: "It seemed to me that his mental reasoning is very _____"

A. mysterious, very curious.

B. simple, very childlike.

C. disturbing, very, very disturbing.

D. deep, very profound.

ANSWER: D. Bush had said of Putin a month earlier, "I looked the man in the eye. I found him to be very straightforward and trustworthy. We had a very good dialogue. I was able to get a sense of his soul." So he kind of owed him one.

5. George W. Bush's nickname for Russian president Vladimir Putin is "Vlad the Impaler." TRUE OR FALSE?

ANSWER: False. He calls him "Pootie-poot."

6. How did George W. Bush characterize America's relationship with Israel?

A. "A delicate balance that requires constant monitoring."

B. "One of the most important international relationships we have."

C. "Their future and ours are inextrably linked."

D. "They're our buddy."

ANSWER: D.

Our Friend to the North

7. What was Canadian prime minister Jean Chretien's response to his spokesperson Françoise Ducros calling George W. Bush a "moron"?

A. He pulled out a photo of Bush reading an upside-down book and said, "She may have a point."

B. He said, "She calls me 'Cretin.' Do you see me getting all upset?"

C. He accepted her resignation and said that Bush is "a friend of mine. He's not a moron at all."

D. He pulled out a photo of Bush looking through binoculars with the lens caps still on and said, "You tell me, does he *look* like a moron?"

ANSWER: C.

Europe

8. How is George W. Bush commonly referred to in Europe?

    A. "The Ugly American"
    B. "The Pulpit Bully"
    C. "The Toxic Texan"
    D. "The Treaty Tearer-Upper"

ANSWER: C.

9. Howard Leach, George W. Bush's ambassador to France, doesn't speak French. TRUE OR FALSE?

ANSWER: True.

10. What message to George W. Bush did three Swedish protesters mooning side by side spell out on their exposed buttocks?

    A. "Bush is an ass."
    B. "We hate Bush."

C. "Bush didn't win."

D. "Hey Bush, stop executing retarded people."

ANSWER: B.

11. On the day of George W. Bush's arrival in Madrid, the newspaper *El Pais* ran an article with the headline "Bush Wins Europe Over One Country at a Time." TRUE OR FALSE?

ANSWER: False. It did, however, run an article about Bush that day with the headline "No One Has Ever Bothered More People in Less Time."

12. What happened at George W. Bush's meeting with Pope John Paul II?

A. He greeted him, "Hey! Holy Man!"

B. He called him "Sir" instead of the rather more respectful (and traditional) "Your Holiness."

C. He said to him, "Come on, what's the truth here? Do people who don't believe in Jesus get to go to Heaven or not?"

D. The pope asked him if he thought God thought he'd really been elected.

ANSWER: B.

13. When a child in London asked him what the White House was like, George W. Bush responded with an impromptu ten-minute description of dozens of the historical rooms. TRUE OR FALSE?

ANSWER: False. He replied, "It is white." And really, what more is there to say?

Danger

14. Who is John Brady Kiesling?

A. The twenty-two-year career diplomat whose resignation letter to Secretary of State Colin Powell said, "Throughout the globe, the United States is becoming associated with the unjustified use of force. The president's disregard for views in other nations, borne out by his neglect of public diplomacy, is giving birth to an anti-American century."

B. The fifteen-year career diplomat whose resignation letter to Secretary of State Colin Powell said, "I strongly believe that going to war now will make the world more dangerous, not safer. . . . Our policies have alienated many of our allies and created ill will in much of the world. . . . I do not believe in the policies of the administration and cannot defend or implement them."

C. The member of George H. W. Bush's administration who said of the Iraq situation, "We have mishandled the diplomacy—if you want to call it diplomacy—monstrously."

D. The twenty-year career diplomat whose resignation letter to Secretary of State Colin Powell said, "Until this Administration it had been possible to believe that by upholding the policies of my president I was also upholding the interests of the American people and the world. I believe it no longer."

ANSWER: D. John H. Brown is the twenty-two-year diplomat. Mary Wright is the fifteen-year diplomat. Lawrence Eagleburger was Bush's father's secretary of state. And Kiesling had much more to say: "The policies we are now asked to advance are incompatible not only with American values but also with American interests. . . . We have begun to dismantle the largest and most effective web of international relationships the world has ever known. . . . We have not seen such systematic distortion of intelligence, such systematic manipulation of American opinion, since the war in Vietnam." But as George W. Bush put it with his usual simple straightforward-ness, "For those who urge more diplomacy, I would simply say that diplomacy hasn't worked."

15. What did former White House counterterrorism adviser Rand Beers say after resigning because of his belief that the administration is "making us less secure, not more secure"?

A. "The difficult long-term issues both at home and abroad have been avoided, neglected, or shortchanged and generally underfunded."

B. "Fixing an agency management problem doesn't make headlines or produce voter support. So if you're looking at things from a political perspective, it's easier to go to war."

C. "As an insider, I saw the things that weren't being done"—cybersecurity, port security, infrastructure protection, immigration management—"and the longer I sat and watched, the more concerned I became."

D. All of the above.

ANSWER: D. And his wife added, "This is an administration that determines what it thinks and then sets about to prove it. There's almost a religious kind of certainty. There's no curiosity about opposing points of view. It's very scary."

Quiz #28

The Ninth Hundred Days

Mmmwwaaa!

1. Which resigning member of his administration received a kiss on the top of the head from George W. Bush?

A. Christie Todd Whitman, EPA administrator
B. Ari Fleischer, press secretary
C. Mitch Daniels, budget director
D. Martin E. Sullivan, chairman of the President's Advisory Committee on Cultural Property

ANSWER: B. Sullivan's departure was not designed to elicit a presidential peck on the head, as his resignation was a protest against the failure of the U.S. military to protect the cultural heritage of Iraq.

More!

2. "This ain't the end of it—we're going to have some more." Who said it and about what?

   A. George W. Bush about wars in the Middle East.
   B. House Majority Leader Tom DeLay (R-Tex.) about tax cuts.
   C. Dick Cheney about obscenely lucrative government contracts awarded to Halliburton.
   D. An unnamed newspaper copy editor about headlines containing the words "cry" (and "cried" or "crying") and "Wolfowitz."

ANSWER: B. Regarding a last-minute change in the bill depriving millions of poor children of a $400 tax credit, DeLay said, "There are a lot of things that are more important than that." As *New York Times* columnist Paul Krugman suggested, "Maybe he was thinking of the 'Hummer deduction,' which stayed in the bill; business owners may now deduct up to $100,000 for the cost of a vehicle, as long as it weighs at least 6,000 pounds."

Judge Not

Match the Bush judicial nominee with his or her controversial decision or statement that has led to a Democratic filibuster against him or her.

3. Ruled against a woman who claimed her privacy had been violated by the doctor who allowed a drug salesman to hang out in the room with them—and laugh at her—while the doctor examined her breasts.

4. Argued that the Violence Against Women Act was unconstitutional.

5. Consistently ruled to make it more difficult for employees to file discrimination suits against employers, for teenagers to get abortions without parental consent, and for the public to get its hands on information the government wants to keep secret.

6. Believes that "the wife is to subordinate herself to her husband . . . the woman is to place herself under the authority of the man," and that people who subscribe to the "feminist principle" of equality of the sexes "are contributing to the culture of death."

   A. James Leon Holmes
   B. William Pryor
   C. Carolyn Kuhl
   D. Priscilla Owen

ANSWERS: 3-C, 4-B, 5-D, 6-A.

Toppling

7. What was a likely contributing factor to George W. Bush's stumbling off his Segway scooter?

   A. His joking efforts to "turn this sumbitch to the far right."
   B. The tennis racket in his right hand that kept him from holding the controls properly.
   C. His being out of sorts as a result of having given up sweets.

D. His mind went to all the criticism he'd gotten for his "Top Gun" landing on the aircraft carrier, and he found himself getting more and more pissed off—How *dare* they make fun of him like that? *Who did they think they were, anyway?*—and then he stumbled.

ANSWER: B.

8. According to an aide who was present at the historic moment, what did George W. Bush say when he saw on TV Saddam Hussein's statue toppled in Baghdad?

A. "Dad, that's how it's done."
B. "Mission accomplished."
C. "They got it down."
D. "Bring 'em on."

ANSWER: C. Well, he wasn't wrong.

Tax Cuts

9. Before George W. Bush delivered a speech in Indianapolis touting his economic policies, his aides asked people in the crowd behind him to take off their ties so they would seem more like the kind of average people Bush deceptively claimed would derive great benefits from his tax cuts. TRUE OR FALSE?

ANSWER: True.

10. House Republicans rejected a Democratic proposal to spend an extra $5 billion on homeland security, to have been paid for by reducing the tax cut for 200,000 of the wealthiest Americans by $25,000 each. TRUE OR FALSE?

Headlines

11. Which headline *did not* appear in a daily U.S. newspaper during George W. Bush's ninth hundred days?

A. "U.S. Jobless Rate Increases to 6.4%, Highest in 9 Years"
B. "EPA: Few Fined for Polluting Water; Agency Says It Must Do Better Job of Monitoring"
C. "White House Cuts Data on Warming in an EPA Report"
D. "Ashcroft Asks to Have Power Curtailed; Says, 'I'm Starting to Scare Myself' "

Touché

12. While playing golf, George W. Bush brandished a golf club like a sword at a reporter and barked, "When I say I'm not answering questions, it means I'm not going to answer questions." TRUE OR FALSE?

Survivor

13. Speaking about President Clinton, George W. Bush's chief of staff Andrew Card said, "Thankfully we have a very strong country that survived his leadership." What did the country "survive" under Clinton?

A. The creation of over 18 million new jobs, the highest level of job creation in U.S. history.
B. The lowering of interest rates leading to the greatest housing boom in U.S. history.
C. The longest sustained economic expansion in U.S. history.
D. All of the above.

ANSWER: D.

Funny

14. Which comic not only announced his support for George W. Bush but also performed at fund-raisers?

A. Chris Rock
B. Dennis Miller
C. Bob Odenkirk
D. Larry David

ANSWER: B. And the funniest thing about it is imagining Bush sitting there listening blankly to those tedious routines packed with arcane pop culture references ungettable even by the hip.

15. How did George W. Bush describe his wife, Laura?

    A. "My much better half."
    B. "The only woman I've ever loved."
    C. "The cream in my coffee."
    D. "The lump in the bed next to me."

ANSWER: D. Awwwww.

Quiz #29

Iraq

Bush Comes to Shove

1. The decision to go to war with Iraq was reached, according to a White House source as quoted by the *Financial Times,* because "a tin-pot dictator was mocking the president. It provoked a sense of anger in the White House." TRUE OR FALSE?

ANSWER: True.

2. What did George W. Bush do immediately before delivering the speech announcing that the United States was at war with Iraq?

   A. He crossed himself and said, "I pray I'm doin' the right thing here."
   B. He winked at Laura and blew her a kiss.

C. He pumped his left fist and declared, "I feel good."

D. He threw up.

ANSWER: C.

3. Which member of George W. Bush's team did Desert Storm commander Norman Schwarzkopf imply he was not too big a fan of?

    A. Secretary of State Colin Powell
    B. Secretary of Defense Donald Rumsfeld
    C. National security adviser Condoleezza Rice
    D. George W. Bush

ANSWER: B. Said Stormin' Norman, "Candidly, I have gotten some-
what nervous at some of the pronouncements Rumsfeld has made."
As for Rumsfeld's sudden ubiquitousness on television, Schwarzkopf
said disapprovingly, "He almost sometimes seems to be enjoying it."

Shock and Awe

4. What about George W. Bush's attitude as he prepared to take the nation into war made an impression
on MSNBC's Chris Matthews?

    A. His "serenity in the face of adversity."
    B. His "obvious reverence for life, even as he knows
that some will be lost."
    C. His "virtually preternatural ability to answer
hostile questions good-naturedly."
    D. His "almost giddy readiness to kill."

ANSWER: D.

5. What did Senate Minority Leader Tom Daschle say "saddened, saddened" him about George W. Bush?

A. "That the president of this great nation acts like such an infant with other countries."
B. "That the president has not a clue of what he's getting himself into in Iraq."
C. "That the president failed so miserably at diplomacy that we are now forced into war."
D. "That a huge percentage of the American people don't dare comprehend what a truly awful president he is."

ANSWER: C.

6. What was George W. Bush's explanation for having traveled to the aircraft carrier USS *Abraham Lincoln* by fighter jet to declare that "major combat operations in Iraq have ended"?

A. Karl Rove said that footage of him in his bomber jacket and helmet would make for some "kick-ass" campaign ads.
B. He wanted to make up a little bit of the year of National Guard flying that he'd skipped out on three decades earlier.
C. "That's where the 'Mission Accomplished' sign was."
D. First he said the ship was too far out to sea to get there by helicopter. Then, when it turned out the ship had been so close to shore that they'd had to struggle to find a camera angle that didn't show the San Diego coastline, he said he'd wanted to

experience the same kind of landing the fighter pilots did.

7. "It is an affront to the Americans killed or injured in Iraq for the president to exploit the trappings of war for the momentary spectacle of a speech. I do not begrudge his salute to American warriors aboard the carrier *Lincoln,* for they have performed bravely and skillfully, as have their countrymen still in Iraq. But I do question the motives of a desk-bound president who assumes the garb of a warrior for the purposes of a speech." Who rose in the Senate to offer this denunciation of George W. Bush's "Top Gun"–like tail-hook landing?

A. Senator Robert Byrd (D-W.Va.)

B. Senator John Kerry (D-Mass.)

C. Senator Joseph Lieberman (D-Conn.)

D. Senator John Edwards (D-N.C.)

8. "I have a message for the president: Enough of the phony, macho rhetoric." Who said it in response to

George W. Bush's taunt to anti-American forces in Iraq to "Bring 'em on"?

A. House Minority Leader Richard Gephardt (D-Mo.)

B. Senator Frank Lautenberg (D-N.J.)

C. Senator Joseph Lieberman (D-Conn.)

D. Reverend Al Sharpton.

ANSWER: A. Lautenberg said, "I am shaking my head in disbelief. When I served in the army in Europe during World War II, I never heard any military commander—let alone the commander in chief—invite enemies to attack U.S. troops."

9. "You all are reporting a lot about some demonstrations, and yeah, there's some demonstrations. That's the first step in a democracy—you're allowed to disagree. Damn, fellas, we ought to be beating our chests every morning. We ought to look in the mirror and get proud and suck in our bellies and stick out our chests and say, 'Damn, we're Americans,' and smile." Who thus admonished reporters to be more positive in their war coverage?

A. Secretary of Defense Donald Rumsfeld

B. Lt. General Jay M. Garner (U.S. Army, Ret.)

C. Lt. General John P. Abizaid (U.S. Army)

D. General Tommy R. Franks (U.S. Army)

ANSWER: B.

10. Private Jessica Lynch sustained multiple gunshot wounds in a to-the-death gun battle with Iraqi soldiers. TRUE OR FALSE?

ANSWER: False. Neither, as unnamed military sources also erroneously claimed, did she sustain stab wounds as Iraqi soldiers closed in—she actually got all of her injuries (broken arm, two fractured legs, dislocated ankle, and head cut) when her army vehicle overturned. Oh, and the stories about how Iraqi doctors ignored Lynch? Not true. U.S. doctors who examined her afterward confirmed that she was well cared for. Also untrue, according to the doctors who treated her, was the story that she was slapped by an Iraqi officer. Finally, as for the great derring-do required for the storming of Saddam Hussein Hospital to effect her rescue in the face of heavy fire, well, there was actually no resistance, since not only had her captors long since fled the scene, but hospital personnel had so informed U.S. forces days earlier.

11. How did American Enterprise Institute scholar Michael Ledeen sum up the war with Iraq?

A. "Mission accomplished!"

B. "Considering that the reason given for the whole thing was to prevent the spread of weapons of mass destruction, you'd think we would have made it more of a priority to protect nuclear facilities against the looting of radioactive material."

C. "The big story isn't that they hyped the evidence to get the country behind the war. The big story is how unprepared they were for what came after."

D. "Every ten years or so, the United States needs to pick up some crappy little country and throw it against the wall, just to show the world we mean business."

ANSWER: D.

WMD

12. How long before George W. Bush made his false State of the Union claim about the Iraq-Niger uranium connection ("The British government has learned that Saddam Hussein recently sought significant quantities of uranium from Africa") had that story been debunked by the CIA?

   A. Three hours
   B. Nine days
   C. Six weeks
   D. Ten months

ANSWER: D.

13. Which headline *did not* appear in a daily U.S. newspaper?

   A. "Some Iraq Analysts Felt Pressure from Cheney Visits"
   B. "Bush Certainty on Iraq Arms Went Beyond Analysts' Views"
   C. "Iraq Weapons Data Flawed, Congress Told; 'We Were All Wrong,' Former U.S. Arms Inspector Says"
   D. "Bush Says He's 'So Embarrassed' About Failure to Find WMD"

ANSWER: D. In fact, he crowed, "We found the weapons of mass destruction," though all that had actually been discovered was two trailers that maybe could have been used as biological weapons labs. "And," he continued, "we'll find more weapons as time goes on. But for those who say we haven't found the banned manufacturing devices or banned weapons, they're wrong. We found them."

14. What do engineering experts believe was the likely purpose of the two trailers whose discovery inspired George W. Bush's premature gloating that portable biological weapons labs—that is, "Weapons of Mass Destruction"—had been found in Iraq?

A. They were used to transport the dozens of Saddam Hussein look-alikes around the country.
B. They were used as "dubbing dens" for bootleg DVDs.
C. They were used to produce hydrogen for weather balloons.
D. They were used by Uday and Qusay Hussein to store a small fraction of their pornography collection.

ANSWER: C.

Who said what?

15. "Most analysts assess Iraq as reconstituting its nuclear weapons program."
16. "We believe he has, in fact, reconstituted nuclear weapons."
17. "I don't know anybody in any government or in any intelligence agency who suggested that the Iraqis had nuclear weapons."

A. Dick Cheney
B. CIA director George Tenet
C. Defense Secretary Donald Rumsfeld

ANSWERS: 15-B, 16-A, 17-C.

18. According to *The New York Times,* what was Colin Powell's response when asked if he would have supported the Iraq war if weapons of mass destruction had been known to be a nonissue?

A. "I would have felt better about the whole thing if we'd taken care of bin Laden first."
B. "I have to save something for my book."
C. "Frankly, it was hard enough supporting it as it was."
D. He merely smiled, held out his hand, and said pleasantly, "It was good to meet you."

ANSWER: D.

Quagmire

19. Who said, in the midst of the U.S. occupation, "I think all foreigners should stop interfering in the internal affairs of Iraq"?

A. Donald Rumsfeld
B. Paul Wolfowitz
C. Dick Cheney
D. Condoleezza Rice

ANSWER: B.

20. When nine senators went to the White House to discuss the possibility of making some of the $87 billion for Iraq a loan, they came away stunned at George W. Bush's newfound humility and spirit of compromise. TRUE OR FALSE?

turns into his mother's son, all ill-tempered haughtiness."

"Adversity always turns the president rabbity and mean . . ." he
here to debate it." As *L.A. Weekly* columnist John Powers noted,
and when someone tried to ask a question, he snapped, "I'm not
ing the meeting and declared of their loan idea, "This is bad policy,"

ANSWER: False. Bush actually slammed his hand on the table dur-

21. When a reporter suggested that his administration's refusal to allow France, Germany, and Russia to bid on Iraq reconstruction projects might violate international law, what did George W. Bush sneer and say?

A. "Lawsuits? Bring 'em on!"

B. "Oh, so now I'm a war criminal?"

C. "International law? I better call my lawyer, he didn't bring that up to me."

D. "[That's] a trick question, so I won't answer it."

Iraq?"
a year from now that you will have reduced the number of troops in
ANSWER: C. Bush said **D** when a reporter asked, "Can you promise

22. Following a particularly bloody day of attacks by anti-American forces in Iraq, George W. Bush claimed that this violence was actually a sign of U.S. progress. TRUE OR FALSE?

make on the ground . . . the more desperate these killers become."
more these killers will react," he explained. "The more progress we
ANSWER: True. "The more successful we are on the ground, the

23. After George W. Bush implied that the MISSION ACCOMPLISHED sign on the USS *Abraham Lincoln* was the Navy's idea rather than his advance team's, which Democratic presidential candidate said, "I guess the

192

next thing we're going to hear is that the sailors told him to wear the flight suit and prance around on the aircraft carrier"?

A. General Wesley Clark (U.S. Army, Ret.)
B. Reverend Al Sharpton
C. House Minority Leader Richard Gephardt (D.-Mo.)
D. Senator John Kerry (D.-Mass.)

24. Who is Darryl Dent?

A. The multibillionaire who says defeating George W. Bush in 2004 is "a matter of life and death," and is spending millions of his own dollars to do it.
B. The Pentagon general who likened the war against Islamic militants to a war with Satan.
C. The Pentagon official who said that the U.S. was in for "a long hard slog" in Iraq.
D. The soldier killed in Iraq whose funeral George W. Bush didn't attend, even though it was held only three miles from the White House.

25. After Saddam Hussein was found in his hole, which former Secretary of State wondered, "Do you suppose that the Bush administration has Osama bin

Laden hidden away somewhere and will bring him out before the election"?

A. Madeleine Albright
B. Warren Christopher
C. George Shultz
D. Alexander Haig

ANSWER: A.

Quiz #30

The Tenth Hundred Days

Who?

1. Who is Stephen J. Hadley?

A. The EPA inspector general whose report on the aftermath of the September 11 attacks said that the White House pressured the agency to say New York's air was safe to breathe before all the data was in.
B. The White House national security aide who fell on his sword and took the blame for the inclusion of faulty intelligence in George W. Bush's State of the Union message.
C. The spokesman for the Center for American Progress who said of the Bush administration, "If they said with a straight face that the world was

flat or the sky was orange, they would expect people to accept it, and would question the patriotism of those who didn't."

D. The writer of *DC 9/11: Time of Crisis,* a docudrama in which Timothy Bottoms as George W. Bush bellows, "If some tinhorn terrorist wants me, tell him to come and get me. I'll be at home, waiting for the bastard!"

ANSWER: B. Nikki L. Tinsley is the EPA whistleblower, David Sirota is the spokesman, Lionel Chetwynd is the screenwriter. As longtime Texas Bush scorner Jim Hightower reviewed the film, "Instead of the doe-eyed, uncertain, worried figure that he was that day, Bush-on-film is transformed into an infallible, John Wayne–ish, Patton-type leader, barking orders to the Secret Service and demanding that the pilots return him immediately to the White House."

Who did what?

2. Defended George W. Bush's economic priorities—refusing to roll back even a penny of his hundred-billion-dollar tax cuts for the rich while keeping down spending on child care for mothers trying to get off welfare—by pointing out that "making people struggle a little bit is not necessarily the worst thing."

3. Declared that "the Bush fiscal policy is the worst policy in the last two hundred years."

4. Participated in a phone conversation with Karl Rove in which Rove called Valerie Plame, the CIA agent married to Bush critic Joseph Wilson, "fair game."

5. Said of the Iraq war, "There was no imminent threat. . . . This whole thing was a fraud."

A. Senator Rick Santorum (R-Pa.)

B. Senator Edward Kennedy (D-Mass.)

C. Nobel Prize–winning economist George A. Akerlof

D. MSNBC's Chris Matthews

6. "I said I don't know. Isn't that clear? You don't understand English?" Who said it to a reporter, and regarding which question that he really didn't want to be asked a second time?

A. Dick Cheney about why he keeps claiming Iraq was involved in the September 11 attacks.

B. Donald Rumsfeld about why the Pentagon seemed to have had its influence over the Iraq reconstruction effort reduced.

C. White House press secretary Scott McClellan about why George W. Bush seems to have no outrage over the outing of Valerie Plame.

D. George W. Bush about why he seems to have such a short fuse.

7. Who did George W. Bush describe as "an honest, fabulous person"?

A. National security adviser Condoleezza Rice

B. Press secretary Scott McClellan

C. Russian president Vladimir Putin

D. British prime minister Tony Blair

How Many?

Match the number with what it counts.

8. American jobs lost since George W. Bush took office.

9. Dollars in deferred compensation so far received by Dick Cheney from Halliburton while serving as vice president, despite his claim to have "no financial interest" in the company.

10. Dollars in Dick Cheney's severance package from Halliburton.

11. Americans with no health insurance in 2002, up almost 6 percent from 2001.

12. Stock options in Halliburton still held by Dick ("no financial interest") Cheney.

13. Dollars awarded in no-bid Pentagon contract to Halliburton and its subsidiaries for helping to reconstruct Iraq.

    A. 367,690
    B. 433,333
    C. 2.7 million
    D. 20 million
    E. 43.6 million
    F. Almost 2 billion

ANSWERS: 8-C, 9-A, 10-D, 11-E, 12-B, 13-F.

14. Over the first thousand days of George W. Bush's presidency, what percentage of respondents in the *New York Times* / CBS News Poll have consistently said that they believed the man was not legitimately elected?

   A. 15–20 percent
   B. 25–30 percent
   C. 35–40 percent
   D. 65–70 percent

ANSWER: C.

Huh?

15. What was Homeland Security Secretary Tom Ridge talking about when he referred to an "unusual sequence of events"?

   A. George W. Bush giving a speech designed to raise his poll numbers, followed almost instantly by a plunge in those numbers to their lowest point yet.
   B. Warnings about *increased* hijacking threats being accompanied by stories about budget cuts that would mean *fewer* air marshals aboard commercial flights.
   C. George W. Bush acknowledging that no link had ever been found connecting Saddam Hussein and the 9/11 attacks, even as Dick Cheney continued to insinuate that such a link existed.
   D. George W. Bush taking office with a ten-year budget projection of a $5.6 trillion surplus and needing a mere thirty months to turn it into a $2.3 trillion deficit.

ANSWER: B.

16. George W. Bush told Fox News's Brit Hume that while he does "glance at the headlines," he "rarely" actually reads the newspapers himself because "a lot of times there's opinions mixed in with news," which he clearly finds distasteful, so instead he gets his news from "the most objective sources" he has: "people on my staff who tell me what's happening in the world." TRUE OR FALSE?

ANSWER: **True.** And doesn't that explain everything?

The Nonfans

17. Who is Sally Baron?

A. The author of a book about Donald Rumsfeld who wrote that the word that best describes him is "manliness."

B. The reporter for *Gotham* magazine to whom George W. Bush's ex-sister-in-law Sharon revealed that his brother Neil dumped her via e-mail after twenty-two years of marriage.

C. The black Bush judicial nominee who called Roosevelt's New Deal "the triumph of our socialist revolution."

D. The seventy-one-year-old Wisconsin woman who so hated George W. Bush that her death notice included the request that "Memorials in her honor can be made to any organization working for the removal of President Bush."

would-be appeals court judge.

ANSWER: D. Midge Decter is the smitten biographer. The *Gotham*
reporter chose to go with "Anonymous." Janice Rogers Brown is the

18. Who is Jonathan Chiat?

A. The Democratic pollster who said of George W.
Bush's September 7 address to the nation about
Iraq, "This was not a confidence-building speech."
B. The local police chaplain who said of George W.
Bush's decision to go for a noon run in 106-degree
Texas heat, "That's weird."
C. The army general who referred to the ongoing
fighting in Iraq as a "classical guerrilla-type
campaign" after Donald Rumsfeld and his minions
had spent weeks insisting that the attacks on U.S.
troops were anything but "guerrilla"-like.
D. The Bush-hating senior editor of *The New
Republic* who wrote, "I hate President George W.
Bush. There, I said it. I think his policies rank him
among the worst presidents in U.S. history. And,
while I'm tempted to leave it at that, the truth is
that I hate him for less substantive reasons, too. I
hate the inequitable way he has come to his
economic and political achievements and his utter
lack of humility (disguised behind transparently
false modesty) at having done so. His favorite
answer to the question of nepotism—'I inherited
half my father's friends and all his enemies'—
conveys the laughable implication that his birth
bestowed more disadvantage than advantage. . . . I
hate the way he walks—shoulders flexed, elbows

splayed out from his sides like a teenage boy feigning machismo. I hate the way he talks— blustery self-assurance masked by a pseudo-populist twang. I even hate the things that everybody seems to like about him. I hate his lame nickname-bestowing—a way to establish one's social superiority beneath a veneer of chumminess. . . . And, while most people who meet Bush claim to like him, I suspect that, if I got to know him personally, I would hate him even more."

ANSWER: D. Stanley Greenberg is the pollster. Vince Castillo is the police chaplain. John P. Abizaid is the general.

The Hands-On Governor

19. When a reporter told him that Arnold Schwarzenegger's entry into the California recall election was "the biggest political story in the country," George W. Bush jealously huffed, "Oh, I think there's maybe other political stories. Isn't there, like, a presidential race coming up?" TRUE OR FALSE?

ANSWER: True.

20. What happened during George W. Bush's first post-election meeting with California governor-elect Arnold Schwarzenegger?

A. Schwarzenegger told Bush to see if the Constitution said anything about the vice president having to have been born here and joked that, if not, it might be time to say "*Hasta la vista*, Cheney."

B. Schwarzenegger explained to Bush that "Bring 'em on!" didn't really work as a catchphrase because it was wildly inappropriate for a leader to invite an attack on his own troops.

C. Schwarzengger said to Bush, "You were governor of a big state," and asked for some general advice.

D. They agreed that terrorism was great for both of them because it made so many Americans feel that their safety depended on giving power to bullies.

ANSWER: C.

Quiz #31

Bushspeak

1. George W. Bush said three of these things. Which one came long ago from the mouth of Dan Quayle?

   A. "There's an old saying in Tennessee—I know it's in Texas, probably in Tennessee—that says 'fool me once, shame on . . . shame on you. You fool me . . . can't get fooled again.' "
   B. "There is nothing that a good defense cannot beat a better offense."
   C. "We'll be a country where the fabrics are made up of groups and loving centers."
   D. "We've got to have an education system that is next to none."

ANSWER: B.

2. How did George W. Bush refer to the senior senator from Massachusetts?

   A. "Edmund Kennedy"
   B. "Eddie Kennedy"
   C. "Teddedy"
   D. "Theodore Kennedy"

ANSWER: D.

3. George W. Bush said three of these things. Which one came long ago from the mouth of Dan Quayle?

   A. "We've got pockets of persistent poverty in our society, which I refuse to declare defeat."
   B. "We can't have a big thick of bureaucratic rules."
   C. "We will move forward, we will move upward, and, yes, we will move onward."
   D. "There was a good news story in Mississippi. I went down there—it wasn't because of me—it was because of the doctors and the citizens understand the cost of a trial system gone array."

ANSWER: C.

4. Complete George W. Bush's warning to Iraqi soldiers that might be following orders from Saddam Hussein: "When Iraq is liberated, you will be treated, tried, and _____ as a war criminal."

   A. tricked
   B. prosecuted
   C. persecuted
   D. executed

ANSWER: C.

5. George W. Bush said three of these things. Which one came long ago from the mouth of Dan Quayle?

A. "The United States and Russia are in the middle of a transformationed relationship that will yield peace and progress."
B. "I believe we are on an irreversible trend toward more freedom and democracy, but that could change."
C. "The reason I believe in a large tax cut because it's what I believe."
D. "We didn't need any more theory in Washington. We needed people that actually done."

ANSWER: B.

6. Whose children did George W. Bush ask for help on behalf of?

A. "Those who are incarsinated."
B. "The weak and the lame."
C. "The powerless."
D. "The powerful."

ANSWER: A.

7. George W. Bush said three of these things. Which one came long ago from the mouth of Dan Quayle?

A. "We'll prevail because we're a fabulous nation, and we're a fabulous nation because we're a nation full of fabulous people."
B. "If you put your mind to it, the first-time home buyer, the low-income home buyer, can have just as nice a house as anybody else."

C. "Border relations between Canada and Mexico have never been better."

D. "The loss of life will be irreplaceable."

ANSWER: D.

8. Complete George W. Bush's statement: "Clear Skies legislation . . . will significantly reduce smog and mercury _____, as well as stop acid rain."

A. emissions

B. omissions

C. admissions

D. emissives

ANSWER: C.

9. George W. Bush said three of these things. Which one came long ago from the mouth of Dan Quayle?

A. "The goals for this country are peace in the world. And the goals for this country are a compassionate American for every single citizen."

B. "There are people that hide in caves, they hide in kind of the dark corners of society, and they use suiciders as their forward army."

C. "If we find somebody who wants to harm America, who espouses a philosophy that's terrorist and bent, I can assure you we will bring that person to justice."

D. "Quite frankly, teachers are the only profession that teach our children."

ANSWER: D.

10. George W. Bush told an ABC News reporter that he would "probably call a couple world leaders today." TRUE OR FALSE?

11. George W. Bush said three of these things. Which one came long ago from the mouth of Dan Quayle?

A. "There haven't been a morning that haven't gone by that I haven't saw—seen—or read threats."
B. "We are ready for any unforeseen event that may or may not occur."
C. "The suicide bombings have increased. There's too many of them."
D. "My most important job is to defend the homeland, to protect innocent Americans from the deaths of the killers."

12. George W. Bush said three of these things. Which one was written by his father in 1998?

A. "Some of the greatest programs—initiatives—come out of our faith-based programs, or faith-based churches or synagogues or mosques."
B. "The war on terror has nothing to do about oil."
C. "People say: 'How can I help on this war against terror? How can I fight evil?' You can do so by mentoring a child, by going into a shut-in's house and say 'I love you.' "
D. "We should not march into Baghdad. . . . To occupy Iraq would instantly shatter our coalition,

turning the whole Arab world against us. . . . It could only plunge that part of the world into even greater instability."

ANSWER: D.

13. How did George W. Bush refer to Colin Powell's wife, Alma?

A. "Alma Mater is here today."
B. "Condi."
C. "Alma Powell, secretary of Colin Powell, is with us."
D. "The lump in the bed next to Colin."

ANSWER: C.

14. What did George W. Bush say was the difference between Americans and terrorists?

A. "They're evil, we're good."
B. "They're ugly, we're pretty."
C. "They hate things, we love things."
D. "You can't really simplify it like that. There are just too many factors to be considered, too many different things that happen in people's lives for me to be so presumptuous as to make some sweeping generalization."

ANSWER: C. To put it in context: "See, we love . . . we love freedom. That's what they didn't understand. They hate things; we love things. They act out of hatred; we don't seek revenge, we seek justice out of love."

15. Three of these utterances came from George W. Bush. Which one was spoken by an unnamed White

House source who seems almost certain to have been Ari Fleischer?

   A. "These are folks that have hijacked a great religion and then take innocent life. And that's a huge difference between America."

   B. "We're here for have a substanative talk on a lot of issues."

   C. "I am here to make an announcement that this Thursday ticket counters and airplanes will fly out of Ronald Reagan Airport."

   D. "That's how the president speaks."

ANSWER: D.

Quiz #32

The Critics Speak

Who said what about George W. Bush?

1. "Much as I respect Estonia and El Salvador, there is something ridiculous about the list of our 'partners'—a coalition of the anonymous, the dependent, the half hearted, and the uninvolved, whose lukewarm support supposedly confers some moral authority. This is like—oh, I don't know, wresting a dubious election victory in Florida and claiming a mandate. It lacks a certain verisimilitude."

2. "Bush is asserting the right of the United States to attack any country that may be a threat to it in five years. . . . And the right of the president to make that decision on behalf of the United States in his sole discretion. . . . In terms of the power he now claims, without significant challenge, George W. Bush is now the closest thing in a long time to dictator of the world."

3. "Just so you know, we're ashamed the president of the United States is from Texas."

4. "Mr. Bush has contrived to have people the world over see this nation—the nation that created the Marshall Plan and ended the Cold War—as an international menace on matters of security, on the environment, on justice, and on fair trade."

    A. Uncredited *New York Observer* editorial writer
    B. Dixie Chick Natalie Maines
    C. *New York Times* columnist Bill Keller
    D. *Slate* columnist Michael Kinsley

ANSWERS: 1-C, 2-D, 3-B, 4-A.

5. "I really think he's a Renaissance kind of guy, and I've known him for twenty years, and I've never been on a topic where he doesn't know something about it." Who said this about George W. Bush?

    A. White House aide Mary Matalin
    B. White House aide Karen Hughes
    C. National security adviser Condoleezza Rice
    D. White House aide Karl Rove

ANSWER: A.

Who said what about George W. Bush?

6. "I think the Bush administration is doing the best they can do with what they have to work with."

7. "The problem isn't that [Democrats] are on the wrong side of the issues. It's that they are afraid to make a stink about being on the right side."

8. "The sermon ended; people were crying. My mind was boggled. Veronica asked if anyone wanted to come forward for special prayer. No one did. I struggled to keep myself in the chair, like a Jim Carrey character, but I found myself lurching forward. She asked me quietly what I needed, and I whispered that I so loathed George Bush that it was making me mentally ill. She put her arm around me, and the church prayed for me,"

A. *Salon* columnist Anne Lamott
B. Actress Teri Garr
C. *Los Angeles Times* columnist Arianna Huffington

ANSWERS: 6-B, 7-C, 8-A.

Who said what about George W. Bush?

9. "Mr. Bush has behaved like a profligate parent who spends every dollar the family has accumulated, mortgages everything the family owns, and maxes out every credit card he can get his hands on."

10. "Mr. Bush's greatest weakness is that too many people, at home and abroad, smell that he's not really interested in repairing the world."

11. "A steady hand on the helm in high seas, a knowledge of where we must go and why, a resolve to achieve safe harbor. More and more this presidency is feeling like a gift."

12. "This is the worst president ever. He is the worst president in all of American history."

A. *New York Times* columnist Thomas L. Friedman
B. *New York Times* columnist Bob Herbert
C. *Wall Street Journal* columnist Peggy Noonan
D. White House correspondent Helen Thomas

ANSWERS: 9-B, 10-A, 11-C, 12-D.

ACKNOWLEDGMENTS

To list all of the people who have encouraged and sustained me by sharing their dislike of George W. Bush—that is, everyone who's left messages on my answering machine ranging from understated ("I don't really care for the man") to rabid ("Is your TV on? Are you hearing what this smug ignoramus is saying?"), and everyone who's e-mailed me great campaign slogans for the '04 race (my favorites are "Re-Defeat Bush," "George W. Bush: It Takes a Village Idiot," and "Bush/Cheney '04: Thanks for Not Paying Attention!") or moronic Bushisms I might not yet have caught up with ("There's no bigger task than protecting the homeland of our country," "The federal government and the state government must not fear programs who change lives, but must welcome those faith-based programs for the embetterment of mankind," and "You know, the bottom line and this corporate America stuff, is that important? Or is serving your neighbor, loving your neighbor like you'd like to be loved yourself?" to mention just a few) or great Web sites (www.foulds2000.freeserve. co.uk/bushv6.htm, www.glennston.com/antibush/, www.iconad.com/georgebush.html, www. buckfush. com, www.bushorchimp.com, www.dubyaspeak.com, www.smirkingchimp.com/, and homepage.mac.com/ leperous/PhotoAlbum1.html, among many worthy others)—would be to take a page that could be so much better used to poke vicious fun at George W. Bush and use it instead to list all my wonderful friends.

I do want to thank my agent, Geri Thoma, and my editor, Becky Cole, for their enthusiasm for this project. I am especially grateful to Susan Morrison and David Remnick at *The New Yorker* for providing me with such a distinguished forum to bash Bush from. Thanks also to all the columnists and commentators whose observations are quoted herein (most notably, Maureen Dowd, Michael Kinsley, Gail Collins, Molly Ivins, and the staff of *The Onion*). Finally, special thanks to Helen Thomas for just coming right out and saying it: "This is the worst president ever. He is the worst president in all of American history."

Everyone else, you know who you are.

About the Author

PAUL SLANSKY is a humor writer for *The New Yorker*. His work has also appeared in, among other publications, *The New York Observer, Spy, The New York Times Magazine, The New Republic, Newsweek,* and *Esquire,* where he was a longtime contributor to the annual "Dubious Achievement Awards." He is the author of *The Clothes Have No Emperor*, a best-selling book about the Reagan presidency. He lives in Santa Monica, California.